THE BUNNY HOP

The Harvey Sheldon Story and the Bandstand Years

By Jon Sutherland

Bloomington, IN Milton Keynes, UK

AuthorHouse™
1663 Liberty Drive, Suite 200
Bloomington, IN 47403
www.authorhouse.com
Phone: 1-800-839-8640

AuthorHouse™ UK Ltd.
500 Avebury Boulevard
Central Milton Keynes, MK9 2BE
www.authorhouse.co.uk
Phone: 08001974150

© 2006 Jon Sutherland. All Rights Reserved.

No part of this book may be reproduced, stored in a retrieval system, or transmitted by any means without the written permission of the author.

First published by AuthorHouse 12/21/05

ISBN: 1-4259-1031-9 (sc)

Printed in the United States of America
Bloomington, Indiana

Edited by: Pete Kennedy

This book is printed on acid-free paper.

e-mail: harveysheldontv@hotmail.com
website: harveysheldontv.com

Cover Photo: Harvey Sheldon
& Dimples (courtesy of
Temple University archives)
Philadelphia 1952–

HARVEY SHELDON
Dedicates this book to
Vivian, Sam, Beth, Ivy,
Evan, and Deryn

JON SUTHERLAND
Dedicates his work to
Donald Lewis Sutherland
and
Elsie Nell Boots

Contents

PREFACE ix
INTRODUCTION xiii
YOU OUGHT TO BE IN MOVIES 1
THIS IS SCHOOL? I THOUGHT IT WAS AN AUDITION 7
LET'S SCTHOOPE SOME TUCHES 15
PHILLY'S COPS 21
IN THE STREETS 25
UNCLE GENE 31
JUDI 35
PHILLY'S THE PLACE 41
BANDSTAND 49
THE BUNNY HOP 61
HOME SWEET HOME 71
MY MAFIA FRIEND 73
BOB HORN 79
BREAKING OUT 85
THE HARVEY SHELDON BIG BAND 91
LOVE SONGS 99
THE ROAD 117
THE SEARCH 125
REDEMPTION 133

PREFACE

There is an old Yiddish idiom I use when I want to make it clear that I have spoken wisely. The sage expression goes, "From my mouth to God's ears." It means, "What I tell you is the truth as I know it, so help me, God." What you are about to read is a pretty incredible story; it may seem impossible to fathom, but I swear to God as my witness, this is the way it all happened. I have had a wonderfully challenging life, and I want to dedicate this book to the most perfect person God could have created for me: My wife. She has made my life so special. It is only because of her that I can finally tell my story. I love you forever, Viv!

I was lucky to be born into a well-to-do family, but I never took that for granted. I had a lot of great opportunities,, and I worked really hard all of my life in pursuit of my dreams. I, along with Dimple, a.k.a. Erma Eineger/Dedi MacGregor, am the co-creator of the Bunny Hop dance. I made a promise to her that as long as I lived, I would always thank her and make sure she was given proper credit for what she had achieved. Doesn't she look great on the cover? Thank you so much all over again, Dimples, for being a true friend! I hope I have lived up to my promise!

To my teachers in school, I send my belated apologies and condolences. Hey, I was just looking for a laugh! Thanks for letting me hang around, Mr. Kramer at Harrity Elementary School, Mrs. Feinberg at Woodrow Wilson Junior High School, and my teacher Mrs. Singer, my Principal Charles Williams, and my football coach Moe Weinstein at Lincoln High School. I gave them all so much grief, but with their letters of recommendation, they all helped me get into an Ivy League school.

I saw exactly how the original Bandstand radio and TV show were conceived, created, and orchestrated by the great Bob Horn. He was my mentor and a great friend. In my eyes, he is the most underrated and misunderstood person in the history of the music business, and he belongs in the Rock and Roll Hall of Fame.

"Hey," to my high school running buddies. We had some fun, don't ya think? Clay Cohen became deputy mayor of Philly and Gene Feldman made a buck in the plastic biz. Anybody ever hear what ever happened to Dave Brenner? They were my pals at the Hot Shoppe.

Hey, Skipper Dawes, thanks for the spot on Teen Time. "Uncle" Gene Krupa, your skill and showmanship as a drummer were only part of who you were to me. You taught me so much about Jazz, and I loved all the time we spent together. Al White, thanks for teaching me how to dance. I would have spent my life with two left feet if it weren't for you; instead, thanks to you, I ended up dancing on Broadway and on Benny Goodman's TV show.

Eddie Newman, I still laugh when I think of you. Thanks for the gigs. "Hey Gov," yeah you, Governor MacCormick of Massachusetts, thanks for coming on my show and helping me get on the network in two weeks! Billy and Dolly Banks, you hired me and you fired me, but you gave me a shot to sell my *shtick*, and I honor that. Jimmie Komack, thanks for the connections. I would never have met Red Buttons or Benny Goodman without your help. Do you still think John Travolta is better looking than me?

To my Big Band, I say heavenly thanks for your talents, energy, and support, along with your belief in me. We never compromised, did we? We always rocked the world in our own way. Billy Root, Vinnie Tanno, Zoot Simms, John Bonnie, Frank Young, Joe Goldberg, and Richie Kamuca, you were the best! And a special thanks to Robert DuPont for his support in keeping this world class band together against all odds.

I have to say thanks to so many more people. When Jon and I started this project, we met rejection in so many ways, but I must offer my humble praise to those who spent time and effort on my behalf.

Thanks, also, to Ray Anthony, Ann Horn, Leroy Lovett, and Mark Porter.

I've always been a big friend of the press, and I know what their passion and power means to all artists trying to deliver their art. I tip my cap to Frank Bookheiser of the *Philadelphia Bulletin*, *Daily News*, and *The Inquirer*; Steve Feldman of the *Jewish Exponent*; and Stu Bykofsky of the *Daily News*.

I will never, ever be able to adequately express my gratitude to Angelo Bruno. We became brothers forever in a simple ceremony, when he gave me a personal promise, and he helped me in times of need when no one else ever could have. Angelo, I don't know if you are in heaven or hell but you are *kosher* by me!

When I finally got the chance to write my story, there was only one writer who could tell it and make it write quite right, and that was Jon Sutherland. I begged him to write my book. I have known Jon for twenty years, and I have always loved the way he writes. His style is clear and concise, with integrity and passion. I kept telling him he should write books; the man is a library unto himself. He kept telling me there has to be a "real deep" story in me to make my tale work. One day, we sat down on a park bench outside of my daughter's house in Pacific Palisades, and he said, "You have an hour to convince me to write your book." He turned me down three times before, but agreed that day, and we began our journey into time together. I bought him a Yiddish dictionary, and I think he liked what he was getting into. I presented him with an impossible puzzle to put together. Whether my thoughts were a *kasheh*, or if I was *tshepen*, he always figured it out. I treasure his friendship, dearly. I wondered in the beginning if a Catholic boy could write a "Jewish book," but Jon has the patience of Job, and he kicked some *touche*! Way to go, Jonny Boy! I hope you can write forever!

More than anything else, this book will show you why I am so blessed. I dedicate this book to my wife of over forty years: My soul mate, Vivian. Please read on...

Yours truly,

Harvey Sheldon, 12/2005

INTRODUCTION

I first met Harvey Sheldon in the fifties in Philadelphia, when he had a popular radio show, and when Philly was the capitol of the music world. I was promoting new artists and producing records. He was a DJ spinning tunes, and I knew he'd like mine. We hit it off right away. His love of music and lyrics impressed me, and I could tell he had wit and style. He mentioned that he wanted to write songs and that he had a few in the can. I welcomed his efforts, but I did have to show him the ropes. He challenged the structure of my songs, and I told him to get a witness! I was a big fan of Harold Arlen and Rodgers and Hart, who often wrote in an unconventional style. It was reminiscent of the way Jewish cantors composed. When Harvey challenged me, he took my compositions to his cantor, and they agreed with me.

Harvey and I wrote many songs together at my house. Harvey had a crisp, clear, and concise technique that blended perfectly with mine. The way he wrote lyrics reminded me of the way songwriters from Broadway wrote theirs. Unfortunately, the music business was going in a whole new direction, and a great era was ending. I'm convinced that if the record companies would have given us a chance, we would have been a hit-writing team.

I think the reason Harvey "got it" was because he understood the history of music and kept his mind open. Those were some of the best times, and Philly was the place to be.

Harvey and I are very different, and there are a few things we disagree on, but we wrote some great songs together, and we have many more stories to tell. I hope you are able to hear them. Some people wait for things to happen in life, but not Harvey; He's a doer!

Leroy Lovett
Songwriter, composer, arranger for Duke Ellington, Nat Cole, Dinah Washington, composer of ""After the Lights Go Down Low," "All At Once," "As I May," "Can't I?" and Vice President of Creative Music for Motown Records

YOU OUGHT TO BE IN MOVIES

"From this you earn a living?" It's a typical Jewish expression that has torn at my soul for my entire life. As long as I can remember, I have been fascinated by the entertainment business. My mother and grandmother jump-started my interest by taking me to shows on the Yiddish comedy circuit at the Lincoln Theater just south of downtown Philadelphia when I was really young. We frequented Vaudeville shows, and even risqué Burlesque acts at the Troc Theater in Philly. I'd memorize the jokes, many of which were very colorful, and I'd launch them wherever I thought I might get the most attention. I loved the adulation and can honestly say I became quite a ham. In the meantime, I was expected to become a *mensch* and earn a respectable living. I wasn't too interested in becoming respectable; I wanted to be funny on stage, which was my version of success. This would become a battle for me. My calling did not meet my family's expectations, so I ventured forth in my life without a safety net.

My inherent curiosity led me to one of the greatest periods of American popular culture. Philadelphia in the forties and fifties was at the crossroads of a great American music revolution, and I was right in the thick of it. Musically, it was a very special time, as big bands, swing, jazz, rhythm and blues, vocal groups, singers and all sorts of incredible artists vied for the legions of growing music fans. Radio was booming, TV was coming into our living rooms, and Philly was selling more records than any other city in America. Down at 46th and Market Street in West Philly in the WFIL studios, Bob Horn built the radio

Bandstand and turned it into the TV Bandstand where I was a regular and where I became the co-creator of the Bunny Hop, America's most enduring dance. I'd like you to come along with me as I tell my story and share some of my insights and the incredible experiences I enjoyed along the way.

"Come on we're going to a *simcheh* in New York City and we need to look good!"

It was 1940, and that was my mother's way of explaining why we would be shopping for some new clothes for a special occasion. We lived comfortably on the southwest side of Philadelphia in a nice home at 5641 Pemberton Street. My father was a successful businessman and my mother was a typical, doting Jewish mother. My grandparents on my father's side lived across town in south Philly at 401 Catherine Street, where they ran a neighborhood furniture store.

Although it was still during the Depression, our family had fared well financially. In fact, my grandmother bought lots of stock during the stock market crash and made quite a bit of money when the market rose to more normal levels. I was the beneficiary of much of this bounty, and as the first born son in a Jewish family, I was expected to be the next "king," or the leader of the clan, and I was told I'd be groomed for the job. At that time, I thought life was one big punch line.

The big day my mother had been talking about for weeks would be the arrival of my grandmother's sister and her family from Europe. We had a big dinner early in the afternoon and packed jugs of water and other drinks for the hour and a half-long drive. My father drove as my mother, grandmother, whom I ceremoniously called Bubbie, and I piled into the car. Back in those days, there were very few places along the turnpike to stop, mostly just Howard Johnson's, so most people traveling would be careful enough to take along what they needed. I remember our excitement building as the September afternoon sun slowly set. By the time we reached the harbor and parked our car, it was nearly dark.

There was quite a large gathering; thousands had come to the waterfront. The big ship, Normandie, would be landing at Pier 82 in New York City, and the people aboard would change my life forever. Typical of most boats coming over from Europe at that time, it included a large cache of Russian Jews immigrating to the United States, relatives coming to visit, and vacationers returning from their travels. My grandmother's sister, Elizabeth Spivak, along with her husband and their two daughters, were onboard. They brought the majority of their material wealth along with them to start up a new business here in the U.S. People couldn't wire money from one account to another back then, and when most people made huge changes like this, they would physically take their jewelry, money, and anything portable and worthy of currency exchange with them.

The Spivaks had been to America before on business and didn't have to go through Ellis Island again. They boarded the boat as any traveler would, but their mission was more unique. They would come to America, set everything up as best they could, financially, and decide to call for the rest of their family to join them when it was time.

As I looked around, I could see such a diverse collection of people and reasons why they were there. Some came here to pick up their friends or relatives, others were crying in disbelief that they would actually see loved ones again, and some had come to get a glimpse of the big stars that had reportedly been on this ship.

Mary Pickford, America's sweetheart of the movies, was returning from filming a picture in Europe with her husband, the big band leader and movie star, Buddy Rogers. Before radio and television, movie stars were the biggest stars and seemed bigger than life. Mary and Buddy would draw quite a crowd. I got lost in the frenzy and gravitated over to where a live band was performing. It was such a joyous day for so many that a band had actually come down to the waterfront to play. I can still remember the exact configuration: Singer, trumpet, trombone, drums, violin, saxophone, accordion, bass, and clarinet. They played favorites like "Hava Negila," and many upbeat, spirited tunes and Jewish numbers. I often wondered why they were there. Did somebody pay them? Did they volunteer? Maybe they had friends or loved ones on the boat, as well. I never did find out.

I loved the big, brassy music and was dancing along to my heart's content. I was wildly swinging and swirling, going with any movement my brain could conduct for my body. In the bedlam, I had become separated from my parents and was watching the people coming down off the big long planks to the sweet freedom of New York City. Different classes of people were coming out at different times, while

The Bunny Hop

the excitement, happiness, and polite chaos created a loud, peaceful joy. Then I saw her. She looked just like she did on the big silver screen where my mother had taken me to watch her movies. Mary Pickford was beautiful, and Buddy Rogers at her side was ever the distinguished gentleman.

For some reason, Mary had seen me dancing and I had caught her interest. She was known as a keen judge of talent, having discovered Judy Garland by spotting her the same way and putting Judy in her movies. In fact, her reputation included the credit that she was brilliant at spotting precocious young talents. Despite the fans who gathered to see her and get autographs, Mary and Buddy came straight toward me. I kept dancing.

When she finally reached me she said, "Hello," and spotting the perfect time for a dramatic response I answered back, "Nice *touche* babe."

She looked at me oddly and asked, "What does that mean?"

I told her it was Yiddish for, "Nice ass."

She was not insulted at all. Instead, she turned to Buddy and asked, "How come you never give me compliments like that?"

Before she could say anything more, I fired a second shot. "You're a *shaineh maidel*."

She asked what I meant and again. I translated. "It means you're a beautiful lady".

Mary turned to Buddy, this time glaring at him, and gave him some more grief. Here I was, a cocky five year-old chatting up one of the world's most beautiful women, and I was at least two compliments ahead of her husband.

Mary picked me up and looked me in the eyes and she said to Buddy, "I have to put this kid in my movies." I'll never forget the look in her eyes for the rest of my life.

I was born with a rare genetic condition. I have double pupils, and it makes my eyes look cat like. My father had them as well, and I was told it was a one-in-a-million condition. In fact, legend has it that it is a spiritual signal.. She was fascinated by the look of my eyes. All I knew was that I was going to be a movie star!

After a few minutes my mother and father realized where I was and wandered over to meet my new friends. My mother struck up a conversation with Mary while my father introduced himself to Buddy. I tried as best I could to hear what everybody was saying, but in reality I was still sky high about being asked to be in a movie. I was hot stuff! Five years old and I'm already cast to be in a movie with Mary Pickford and Buddy Rodgers, I thought to myself. I couldn't have gotten a bigger break. When Mary finally asked my mother for her permission to take me to California for the filming, my mother asked for a few minutes to talk it over with my father. I remember that Mary even offered to pay for my mother to come out to Hollywood with me. My parents wandered just out of earshot and went back and forth over the pros and cons. I really didn't think there was much to talk about; I had already made up my mind.

When my mother came back from talking to my father, Mary asked her the big question once again, and my mother said, "No."

I was shocked and stunned. I couldn't move. I was paralyzed. I couldn't believe what I had just heard. When Mary and Buddy slowly walked away and out of my life, I felt this giant wall of sadness rush over me. I knew I would never be the same.

THIS IS SCHOOL? I THOUGHT IT WAS AN AUDITION

My grandmother's sister and husband made it off the boat safely and with all of their valuables, and we gathered them up for the trek back to Philadelphia. They had even brought two suits over for me; maybe they had already been tipped off that I was a hot dresser. There was joy and celebration in the air, and I was happy for everybody else, but I now had an emptiness that I had to fill. It may be hard for others to fathom why this hurt me so much, but I knew I had the break of a lifetime, one that may never come again. It was taken away from me, and I didn't understand why. This development in my life would take on physical consequences. I began to stutter, an impediment that became increasingly worse. I went cross-eyed, as well. My mind seemed to be punishing my body for my bad luck. I was miserable, and my parents spent large amounts of money running me around to specialists and doctors who were known to cure these conditions. What they didn't have was a cure for a broken heart.

The Spivaks stayed with us for just over a month, and all the joy that had been seen at the dock was eroded by their arrogant criticism of the United States. Their family had been deposed by Russia over the years, and they eventually settled in France. France was the only place a Jew in Europe could be granted citizenship. (Thanks, Napoleon!) Once there, hard work and frugal business habits made many Jews successful businessmen. The Spivaks had climbed their way up the social ladder, and had lived a very elitist lifestyle afforded to them by their wealth. They saw New York and Philadelphia as a step below that of their adopted Paris, and they were not afraid to say so. I thought that their family's suffering while coming across Europe like gypsies would keep them more grounded and humble. That was not the case. Many Jews in Europe felt the same way, and many did not take Hitler's threats seriously. I can remember my great uncle saying that Hitler did not have the power or the resources to threaten France.

At the end of their month's stay, the Spivaks announced to us that they would be returning to Europe. They insisted on leaving all of their money in their own names and in secure, hidden locations. My father warned them against that. He remarked that if anything ever happened to them, the money would be lost forever and would not be of any use to anyone, especially their children. My Uncle Spivak shook that one off and refused, stating flatly that as a successful man he knew what was best for his family. My father seemed confused by their belligerent ways and told our family that the Spivaks were making a grave mistake and that we should pray for them. He didn't feel they were using sound judgment by chancing a return to Europe. After all, they had plenty of money. It was more than enough to get a new start in America. Instead, they were greedy, and we ended up taking them back to the same port and waving good-bye. The next spring we got word that the Nazis had murdered them all.

None of the therapy and visits to the doctors was doing me any good. I continued to struggle in school, and my attention span was that of a gnat. Most importantly, I didn't want to be there. I already knew what I wanted to do. I wanted to be a comedian like the ones we used to see in the Catskills. But how could I do that if I was stuttering while looking at the audience cross-eyed through the stupid glasses the doctors made me wear? I was at my wits' end, and my mother couldn't think of any other ways to combat my obviously psychosomatic disorder. At that time, Harvey Sheldon wasn't very proud of Harvey Sheldon. In fact, he felt like an idiot.

My grandfather said he could try to help. He was a doctor, but refrained from having any of his family be his patients. According to him, this was going to be a social visit not a professional one. The first thing he noticed while I played was that I didn't stutter when I sang. He pointed this out.

"When you learn songs, don't you have to memorize the lyrics before you sing them?"

"Yes," I said sheepishly.

"So why don't you memorize the things you want to say before you say them? Don't let your brain get too far ahead of your mouth."

I tried his technique. At first it was clumsy, but once I learned to think in that pattern, my stuttering started to dissolve into free and clear speech.

"And as for your eyes," my grandfather said, "Throw away those glasses. They are no good for you. You don't need to put a patch over your eyes to get your eyes stronger. You need to use them! I suggest that you go see movies. They will open your eyes!"

That was like telling a pig to go lie in *drek*. I already watched movies; I'd just needed to do it some more! Now, when I begged to go to the movies over and over again I could tell my mother that it was part of my medical prescription!

I loved the big, old silver screen. It was so dramatic. Television sets weren't available yet, and radio usually only played music late at night. Movies were the best form of entertainment around, and going to theaters took up a large part of my time. I'd watch anything I could, but I particularly felt affection for comedies. As far as I was concerned, the world had room for a lot more jokes, and the Jews had a special affinity for the magical combination of words that cause amusement.

As I grew up I could see how the comedy and entertainment world was of such interest to those of my culture. Jews would gather together naturally, but we didn't have much to do for entertainment, so the rise of Jewish self-deprecating humor was born. One Jew would get up to tell how miserable his life was, and another would try and top it. Then, another would tell his story, but feature a bit more exaggeration, and pretty soon we were the most miserable sons-of-bitches on Earth. But, at least we were having a good laugh, even if it was at our own expense.

I loved the routines and couldn't learn enough of them. I especially liked the ones with the Yiddish punch lines; they seemed to pack a bigger wallop. English is a pretty sturdy language, phonetically, but because Yiddish is a combination of German and Hebrew, it has a very percussive timbre to it. So roll out the sweet talk in English, and let

The Bunny Hop

'em have the hammer in Yiddish. It was the best way to make a Jew laugh through those nights in the clubs. If I had my way, I would've been on that stage at about age six, but there were other things that were more important in our society. If I was supposed to be the king of the Sheldons, I would have to study academics and become a doctor, a lawyer, a scientist, or something respectable. I might aspire to be the next Albert Einstein. I wanted to be like Menasha Skulnick, who was the most outrageous comedian on the whole Yiddish comedy scene.

Needless to say, I wasn't too popular at school with the teachers. I saw school as an audition to try out some of my well-stolen and developed *shtick*. Why should I care about discipline? And if they kicked me out? Hell, I could run away and get a job in the clubs, just like Al Jolson or Eddie Cantor. Somebody had to understand the importance of a six-year old loud mouth with a foul tongue.

I always thought the class loved me, because face it, folks, elementary school in the forties was pretty dry stuff with the war going on and all. So, I figured it needed a little spice. I decided to make amends with a teacher who had found my comedy most disrupting. I brought a present, and offered her the long box, beautifully wrapped, with a ribbon tied into a bow. It was large enough to hold something real nice, like a sweater or a blouse, but when my teacher opened it up, she caught glimpse of a foot-long, frozen rat, courtesy of the streets of Philadelphia. She screamed so loud as she ran out of the room, that teachers from all over the school scurried over to see what the disturbance was.

Once the class got a glimpse of the rat and got over the smell, they could appreciate the joy I was reveling in. She fell for my prank, hook, line, and sinker. Of course I was immediately summoned to the principal's office and suspended, but I knew he was in on the joke because he'd been laughing about the prank when I walked in. My mother saw nothing wrong with what I did when she came to the school and heard what punishment was being handed out. She steadfastly supported me throughout my educational tour of duty because I was getting good grades. Had I been flunking out, maybe she would have had more of an opinion against me, but it seemed perfectly normal to her; I acted the same way at home.

In those years, we had an early morning period for prayer. It was usually just a minute or two when the kids of each faith would gather and mumble a few prayers, look bored or try to grab a nap. I made a spectacle of myself one morning by making exaggerated motions while getting into position to pray. The girls were giggling at my accordion like gyrations when the teacher finally singled me out. "What are we doing Mr. Sheldon?"

I liked being called "Mr. Sheldon," and it helped set up my joke.

"I'm just laying *tefhelen*."

She put her hands on her hips and asked me, in front of the whole class, what exactly I had said, for those who didn't speak Yiddish.

"I said, 'I'm getting laid!'"

"That's it, Harvey Sheldon! You're done for the day!" She dragged me out of the class for another lecture while all the kids were laughing.

"I'm telling you the truth," I begged as I was getting a personal escort through the hallway. "Laying *tefhlen* means I am getting prone, lying down to pray. I'm getting laid." Instead of sympathy, I got another dose of detention.

Pretty soon I had carved out my territory. Most teachers knew of my reputation. They either learned to indulge me or try to avoid me altogether. But the teachers who had the nerve to call on me to answer questions got a handful! In a thoroughly boring musical class our teacher kept *shmoozen* the virtues of Bach and asked me what I thought about it.

"Can't dance to it." I said. "The man has no rhythm!"

She insisted that classical music was something you must acquire a taste for, to which I blurted out, "Do you have to acquire a taste for sex?"

The class roared with laughter, and this time I was suspended for profanity.

A couple of days later I had still not learned my lesson. This time an unsuspecting teacher had the gall to ask us what we did over the weekend. After a couple of students shared boring stories about family outings, I busted loose. I told the teacher that I had gone to a show where I'd seen a *shaineh maidel* with a body like a coke bottle and with a *touche* that only *got vaist* what it is like. The class roared with approval, because the Jewish students were all well-versed in Yiddish, and the Italians that made up most of the rest of class knew the teacher was at least being made fun of, even if they didn't understand my language. I

The Bunny Hop

got singled out, and other teachers came in to quell the hysteria, but my poor teacher tried to repeat what I said. Instead of support, she drew laughs from the other teachers who knew the lingo and understood what I had said. I had told her I saw a lady with a coke bottle figure, and only God knew what her ass was like. To make things even better, I got kicked out of school again!

Getting suspended really wasn't much of a deterrent, because every time I'd get the boot I had to be back in class the next day at 8:00AM. I think I showed enough merit that they evidently felt it was worth keeping me in school and not worth shipping me off to another district. When we had talent shows, I would really bust out my "A" material, and the crowds loved it. Those shows generated a lot of money for wartime causes and that earned me some points. My jokes and acting skill had just landed me a role in a Broadway review and the school knew it. The entertainers from those shows were keen to see me perform, and it gave me a safety net for my insidious pranks and tomfoolery at the expense of a proper education. I didn't need a proper education. What I needed was to remember my punch lines and time them just right.

I never felt low on material, but good inspiration was always useful. Whenever I could get a ticket to go to a Burlesque show or to Vaudeville, I'd be the first in line. There were only two remaining theaters in Philly that still catered to that audience. One was the Earl And Erlanger Theater and the other was The Mastbaum. My favorite skit at the time was by Billy Hagen, a.k.a. "Cheese & Crackers," who would come on stage to give the audience a geography lesson using a topless model for his demonstration. The moral of that skit was not lost on me!

There was one teacher named Skinny Miller. She had purple hair and dressed like somebody out of the civil war. She knew I was not in school the day before. I had ditched. I was doing research at the burlesque show! So trying to humiliate me, thinking I wouldn't know the lesson from the previous day, she called on me to come to the blackboard and tell us what I had learned yesterday. The teacher walked to the back of the room to get a full view of my destruction.

Confidently, I waltzed to the chalkboard and quickly drew the silhouette of a naked lady.

"I learned a geography lesson yesterday!" I said proudly. I pointed to the left breast and said, "This is the Appalachian Mountains." I pointed to her belly button and said, "This is the mid-west." Pointing to her right breast I continued, "And this is the Rocky Mountains."

The class was in stitches, and the teacher got there just in time to stop me from showing them how to go cross-country.

I meant no harm in any of these pranks, because I knew they were silly and helped lighten the load. I just couldn't stop myself. I felt compelled to get a laugh. If I saw an opening, I had to capitalize on my opportunity. Sure I was punished, and in most cases rightly so, but I knew there was no school for comedy or show business you could go to, so I made up my own. I thought I was making very creative use of my educational activities. Outside of school, all bets were off. I had no net. Then, I really went for it.

LET'S SCTHOOPE SOME TUCHES

When I was nine years old, Bill McCoy married my godmother's sister, Elizabeth Abrams, making him my uncle. He was not Jewish, and it was highly frowned upon when anybody married into the family from outside of the faith. It was suggested that by doing so, the offender was losing half of his or her soul. I really liked Bill. He had been one of the original Philadelphia Eagles when that franchise was first founded, and he played for six years in the NFL. Football players in those days weren't as big as they are now. There was no specialization so players had to go "both ways" by playing offense and defense. They seemed much more like everyday people than the behemoths you see in the NFL on Sundays now.

Bill got the head-coaching job for the West Catholic High School football team, and I enjoyed going by to watch the team work out. I loved the action, all of intricate plays, and the whole scenario of practicing and then going full blown in the games. Pretty soon, I was hanging out with the team all the time, and I even got to go to their team meetings.

In those days, the high school football games were often the biggest sporting event of the whole week. The entire town would be absorbed by these contests between rival towns and neighborhoods. As a regular, I would try to make myself useful during the practices, which also meant I was missing my Hebrew lessons. When classes were over, I was expected to attend Hebrew School on the long road to getting Bar

Mitzvahed. At that time I think I knew more about football than I did my religion, and I was having a blast.

The bigger kids in those days were the Poles, and they were quite comfortable with the violent world of amateur football. But, there was a mixture of cultures on this Catholic football team. Obviously, there would be Italians because they were all Catholic, but there were also Greeks and other European descendants. There were no Jews playing in the league, but the team had my support! My uncle had built a really good team, and I was proud to be around them.

When the first game came up, I went down and walked right into the locker room and no one stopped me. My reputation had preceded me a bit, and I was told to behave. Brother Joseph, the school's priest, was there to lead the team in prayer before the opening kick-off. We all gathered in a tight circle and I stood next to my friend Bruno, a tough Italian kid who was really friendly to me. I caught on to his slang and he recognized a lot of my *shtick*. Since the Jews and Italians were so friendly, most of the Italians knew a fair bit of Yiddish. When Brother Joseph gave his final blessing to all the players, there was a moment of silence, and feeling a desperate need to give my team support I spouted out *"mazal tov!"* Bruno laughed as the rest of the team looked at me in complete indignation.

The starting quarterback Charlie Albertus yelled out, "What the hell is so funny?"

Bruno politely just said, "It means good luck, and a celebration is coming!"

I felt a great deal of relief when all of the people in the room started laughing and knew I really meant it. Even Brother Joseph couldn't help from laughing along with the team.

As everybody walked toward the field I could hear my Uncle Bill telling my aunt Elizabeth, "Next time keep him quiet," but the players loved it because it broke the rigidity of the locker room silence.

West Catholic High School was roughing up a team they had never beaten before, and there was a tension that felt odd. I kept wondering why the guys were playing so great but looking so glum. I figured that maybe they just thought they were lucky. I knew they were a really good team, though. Uncle Bill was doing his best to keep the team pepped up, but you could hear the trepidation in his voice. Maybe he

LET'S SCTHOOPE SOME TUCHES

didn't believe the team's good fortune and felt a need to implore his players not to let up. After the pre-game locker room incident, I was told to put a sock in it, but I knew any good entertainer is only as good as his last gag.

As my uncle paced back and forth I could see his wife just cringe as I started to talk with my friend, Bruno. Once again, Bruno laughed out loud, and my uncle turned to look at us as if to punish us for talking while he was speaking to the whole team.

"What did the kid say?"

He shook his hand at me and was acting as if this would finally shut me up. He asked Bruno to translate once again. You could hear a pin drop, but I had a shit-eating grin on my face.

I said to Bruno, "You *schtooped their tuches* in the first half, so keep *schtooping their tuches* and you will win, as God is my witness!"

I knew if I threw God into the equation in this Catholic environment, it would enhance my chances of getting heard.

Bruno stood up and said,. "The kid said, 'We're kicking their asses, and if we keep kicking their asses, we will win!'"

That was exactly what the team wanted to hear. They weren't sold on the fire and brimstone Uncle Bill was delivering; they just wanted to have some fun. The team was fired up because they knew a nine-year old Jewish kid could see the West Catholic Eagles were giving somebody a real Sunday licking.

They exploded back onto the field and I heard Brother Joseph say, "I've never seen you get the team this excited Bill. Maybe the kid has something, there."

I know that was a confusing message to Uncle Bill. I was stealing some of his thunder, but if he really wanted the team to win he sure could use my support. I had all sorts of inspirational messages I could yell out at the team from the end of the bench to keep them pumped up.

West Catholic completed the demolition by a score of 45 to 13, and when the victorious team came back to the locker room, they demanded that I be at all the prayers and games. Brother Joseph was speechless.

Uncle Bill was beside himself not knowing what to think when Bruno piped up, "Coach, the little Jewish kid fires us up."

Even Charlie Albertus, the hot shot quarterback was on my side saying, "We need him, Coach, he brings us good luck."

They even said that they wanted to hear the Jewish prayers I'd been saying before the game.

Brother Joseph was befuddled. "What's the Pope going to think? I have a Catholic high school who wants to hear Jewish prayers before the football game!"

I knew I had the gig.

The team was catching on really well. Most of them understood my Yiddish slang well, by now. *"Let's schtoope their touches!"* (kick their asses) became a real rallying cry. They also performed very well to some of my unprintable, favorite sayings.

Before you knew it, West Catholic High School was 4-0 and looked like a real football powerhouse for the first time in years. I loved my new audience and reveled in the attention. Uncle Bill was a lot more comfortable with the situation and was giving me a lot of confidence, as well. Our fifth game was against Roman Catholic High School, who had been a powerhouse for years. They were definitely going to be our toughest opponent of the whole season. Then, I blew it. I spilled a whole bottle of black ink on the carpet at home and, for punishment, I was not allowed to go to the game.

It was torture. The game was played at Shibe Park, the home of the NFL Philadelphia Eagles and the Philadelphia Athletics. 25,000 people showed up and most of them knew it could be the deciding game on the way towards the city championship. I refused to eat all day, and I was completely miserable. I never left my room.

I had a little radio so I could listen to the game and I rooted as hard as I could for the guys, even though I couldn't be there. I sincerely believed that without me being there the team would lose, and it would be my fault. It was like a living a nightmare that very easily could have been prevented, had I just not been such a clod! The team was flat offensively and defensively, and the broadcast of the game seemed to last for ages. The most painful moment came when I heard my own name on the radio, as the announcer told everyone that West Catholic's mascot was mysteriously missing. I was in tears when we lost. I never meant to drop that bottle; it was an accident. Honest! It wasn't part of a prank that went wrong. It was just a mistake, but I guess I'd pressed my luck just one too many times, and it was the only way my parents could get my attention.

During the next week I felt ashamed and didn't go around to the practices as usual. I even made it to a couple of my Hebrew lessons like I was supposed to. Those classes were such a drag. Instead of being out and playing ball or chatting up girls, we were supposed to be doing Bible study and leaning more about the Torah. I wanted to hear new music and go help the team as much as I could.

I really wanted to see the guys on the team, but I was afraid they would think I let them down. Little did I know that Brother Joseph had come around to see my Rabbi. He had confided to my Uncle Bill that the team really needed me there and looked lost without me. My Rabbi was well aware of my interesting outside activities. Brother Joseph asked his permission that I might be able to return to the team, but with a little more humility. He mentioned that at times my language, when translated, was a bit obscene. The good Rabbi reminded Brother Joseph that many famous Catholics, like Joan of Arc, had foul mouths and it wasn't the actual language that was important. It was the spirit of the language. The soul of the words was the essence. In his own way, he was saying that the Jews don't spend as much time worrying about who they might offend by brusque language, as long as the truth gets heard. While giving his blessing the Rabbi said, "One day you or yours will be paying a lot of money to see Harvey Sheldon perform. He has a natural talent for making people laugh, and you should just let that be. He has *chutzpeh*; it's his gift from God. You'll find there is a medicinal spirit to laughter. We all need it. I pray the government won't require a prescription for laughter in the future."

I was welcomed back with friendly pats on the head and handshakes all around, but I still felt like I hadn't done enough. As the team listened to Brother Joseph's final prayers before our next game, I could sense the silence. I knew everybody wanted me to say something to get everybody in the mood. I hadn't consciously written a speech I just started speaking to no one in particular.

"You are about to face a *phakata* team."

Bruno interpreted. "We're facing a shitty team."

"Last week you played like *drek*!

"Last week we played like shit!"

The Bunny Hop

"Now lets get out there and beat the *drek* out of them!"

And just as I was to remind the whole team of their mission, they had a cheer for me to lift my spirits.

The whole team yelled out, "Let's *schtoope some tuches*!"

It was like I never left, only better.

Brother Joseph came over to me, obviously happy that his team was all pumped up, but still concerned about what he considered profanity. I stated my defense by repeating a lesson I actually learned from a Rabbi. The Rabbi once told me that the Oxford dictionary was created by an American doctor who was in a mental institution. Because of it, he may have left out a few words we like to use! Brother Joseph just shook his head as I escaped the noose one more time.

We *schtooped the tuches* of that *phakata* team, and beat the living *drek* out of them. We ran the table all the way to the city championship game where, just for fun, we rubbed it in. In the championship game the other team seemed to know our plays too well, so I suggested to Uncle Bill that we should call our plays in Yiddish. After all, we were the only Catholic school in the league that knew the language, so we had this incredible advantage. We drew our opponents off-sides by barking out "*drek, phakata, shctoope tuche, hike*!" Instead of saying "on two" in the huddle, we'd say "on *drek*." We really got inside their heads, and they lost all of their composure. They even got called for un-sportsmanlike conduct for swearing at us during the game, because they were so frustrated by our Yiddish signals. It was a cakewalk. West Catholic High School was City Champs, and I couldn't have been prouder.

PHILLY'S COPS

As I got a little older, the world got bigger and better, but more difficult.. As a kid, I could pretty much be sure I would have fun. It wasn't until I got a better glimpse of the adult world that I realized how screwed up this place can be, and how Jews have been affected.. My parents warned me of what I would see, but I didn't really get it until I saw it first hand. I knew being Jewish was a problem for some people, but not for me. I loved being Jewish, but over and over again I could see roadblocks that I felt were either unfair or created just to make our lives more difficult. The entertainment world I wanted to be in was filled with talent from all races and colors. I saw that the day-to-day grind in which most people participate is not that romantic; in fact, it was quite ugly. I didn't really understand why people could want to live that way, and I certainly didn't like any injustice I saw. I learned the pre-judgment that is prejudice is real. It's very sad but it's real.

Since my father was so successful, we could afford a fine life. My parents went out to dinner at least two or three nights a week and frequented nightclubs, and I knew when I got old enough I was determined to double their high-life attendance rate. One morning, we were out for breakfast at Horn & Hardart in downtown Philadelphia. We were dining leisurely, and I even had the nerve to ask for dessert after breakfast. I ordered a luscious piece of coconut custard pie, and was ready to enjoy it thoroughly, when a couple of Philly's finest (we used to call them Philly's worst because they were so anti-Semitic) cops came into the restaurant.

Somehow the two officers who walked in felt compelled to make a spectacle of us. The lead cop made an off-the-cuff remark that I'm sure he wanted every one in the room to hear. "You God-damned Jews want to have the best of everything."

I thought "Well, yeah. Who doesn't?"

Then he continued, "You even got the last piece of coconut custard pie that is always saved for me."

Before I could get the fork to my mouth and taste that delicious pie, my mother took the initiative. She was totally pissed.

"You want this piece of pie? You can have this piece of pie!" Before the words even carried across the room, she slammed that slice of pie in the cop's face and bedlam was upon us. My father, who was concerned that my mother would be grabbed by the other cop, drop stepped so he could throw an over hand right hay-maker of a punch that flattened the second cop in his tracks. He knocked the cop out cold. My father was a huge boxing fan and had one hell of a punch. Pretty soon, there were cops everywhere, taking my parents away to jail.

For what, being insulted and standing up for ourselves?

I had been implicitly instructed in my youth that if anything ever was to go wrong in our family, I was to immediately call my uncle Harvey Kolodner, who was a judge in the Federal District Court of Appeals. If he wasn't there, I had to keep calling over and over again until I could speak to him. He was a Federal Judge with incredible connections and had enormous, unseen powers. He'd been the chief speechwriter for President Roosevelt and was a very highly respected man. He was my family's protection blanket wherever we went.

In an hour, both of my parents were back home and those cops were in deep *drek*. I would see this scenario play out many more times. My mother had no room for any intolerance and had the *chutzpeh* to back it up. My father was ever ready to work against any resistance he met, but so many times I felt like it was just us against the world. We did have a bit of an unofficial safety net. Most of the judges, lawyers, and district attorneys were Jews, so cases like ours didn't get that far. We felt it safer to go straight to the top, right away.

I often wondered what we were doing wrong. My father was an influential, important, and dignified man. My mother was a former Miss Philadelphia, and as smart as a whip. I was always extremely popular in school, and I was steadily growing into my best years. We had it all, but sometimes it felt like we had nothing but a fight on our hands. It just didn't figure. I felt so much safer in the artistic world where it was all about talent, creativity, hard work, and good times for all. To me, society seemed like a child to me that had not really grown up, and I thought I had.

My father never took a vacation from work. It wasn't his modus operandi. We'd have dinners out and weekend getaways, but we did not ever go away for a week or two. There was always business at home to attend to each Monday morning, so we always ended up back at our house and ready to start a new week. It made those weekends away from the house packed with activity. One of our favorite haunts was Atlantic City on the New Jersey shore. It was only an hour away, and there were great night clubs there that my parents loved and where I practically lived when I came of age.

Atlantic City was like a second home for Jews and Italians, but there was one place there that was not. The Army took over a hotel where soldiers who were hurt in World War II came back to rehabilitate. It was right near the beach. I can remember walking by the hotel with my mother. Many of the injured soldiers sat in wheelchairs, but they still had enough energy to yell out anti-Semitic slurs at us. Sadly, there was even a sign on the beach that said "No Jews/No Negroes/No Dogs Allowed."

One day, there was a mini-parade in Atlantic City by the recovery center. Bess Myerson, a Jewish woman we were very proud of, was being honored. I could taste the jeers as someone in the crowd booed. My mom was losing it. After a couple of really off-color remarks, she went up to a couple of the soldiers and started to pick a fight. Quickly, a commanding officer came over to make peace, and he pulled my mother aside. There was some rough sentiment brewing in those days toward many anti-Semitic people who served as soldiers. Ironically, some people thought the anti-Semitic soldiers were fighting World War II to save the Jews. It was a small fraction of those who served that were anti-Semitic, but it still felt really ugly. In their minds, they blamed their injuries on us. My mother confronted a couple of hecklers and gave them a piece of her mind.

"You want to boo her? Then boo me so I can slap your face. You

The Bunny Hop

have so much hatred in your hearts, and you deserve your injuries."

The C.O. did the right thing by defusing the situation, and I overheard him say, "These guys are no patriots. Sure, they fought for us. We are grateful for that, and always will be. We are embarrassed by them at times, but it is our duty to take care of them, so I think it's best that you just move along, and let us handle this."

He seemed so civil, while the aura was so hateful around him. I admired his wisdom and clarity of thought, while he was pinned between a rock and a really hard place.

Well, we allowed ourselves the right to visit the beach and were having a grand old time when another of society's appointed henchmen decided that we weren't worthy of visiting this cove. The cop on the beach was slow to get to his point; mostly, he frothed at us with indignation. I'm sure he was thinking, "How dare these Jews sit on this beach with all that's going on in Europe?"

I was eleven so I wondered how I could be in the service and be shooting at the Germans. My mom was in no danger of being drafted for service. So why couldn't we go to the beach? Are we supposed to hide in our closets until this is all over? We wanted to live the life we had. What's wrong with that?

I could tell I was going to be needed legally, and got ready for my chores. Sure enough, that beach cop pressed my mother one too many times, and she took umbrage. She smacked the cop in the knees with our beach umbrella, and sure enough, I was on the phone getting her bailed out of jail by my uncle, once again.

I got good at this sweet-talking thing. A judge, a teacher; get me anybody on the phone, and I always felt I could get my way. Some may call it B.S., I call it the gift of language, and it has been my salvation since then. Hey, feel free to go check my references, but when you are living your whole life pulling yourself up by the seat of your pants, you tend to remember the details really well.

My parents put up a good front, but I started to see the cracks. As much as they enjoyed Philadelphia society, home became a war-zone. Their arguing increased exponentially. Dad was too busy; Mom was a *balebosteh*. At times I thought they were the perfect couple. The next day, I would wonder how they ever got along at all.

IN THE STREETS

If you throw enough different people into the same area, each is going to carve out his or her turf and try to get comfortable. It's the human condition. That's the way I saw Philly when I was growing up. There were tons of first- and second-generation citizens mixing in with the established population. Of course, each culture is going to want to be with its own, but in a city of that size, mixing and growing are inevitable. Quickly, I got to see the ropes. The Germans didn't want to be around the Jews, but they could tolerate Poles. The Italians had no love for the Germans, but could be very friendly with the Jews. In fact, I used to joke that I never knew an Italian who couldn't sing, or a Jew that would shut-up.

I felt there were a lot of other reasons why the Italians and the Jews got on so well. If you look at the family structure it's nearly the same. They both have the strong, powerful mother who was to be worshipped and the hard working, respected father. Whenever I'd go over to an Italian friend's home, I would be fed and fed and fed. If that same friend came over my house my mother would treat him like her own.

There was one taboo: Dating. Otherwise, we were naturals to work together, and we often did work together in my musical travels later in life. The Irish and the Scots were very polite and comfortable among themselves, and when you dug deep into the psyche of the English immigrants, it was no secret that they were no fans of the Jews. Being Black, sadly, was completely another equation. Discreet, thin little civilized battle lines had been drawn even if most acted as if they didn't exist.

For the life of me, I kept trying to make sense of all this. As I studied in school, I began to take a detour. Of course, I had to read the chapters assigned. I passed my tests, but I wanted to know more. I got into heated debates with teachers over the subject matter taught, but I knew deep down inside that what they were spouting was their gospel. It wasn't mine! There was nothing about Jews, Blacks, or Indians in any of their textbooks. It was a complete W.A.S.P. whitewash, and it bored me to tears.

When the ultimate boredom crept in, I had to get creative. I was either going to do a face-plant on my desk and fall asleep for being out too late the night before, or I had to stir things up. When the history teacher was lecturing, and would name and some significant event, I'd shout out something really bad that happened that same year. It was a real comeuppance I was proud to display. I thought history in high school was the most B.S. course I ever took. It wasn't even close to the truth. I felt it was much more like propaganda, which is another subject into which I'd like to delve.

I have the benefit of hindsight 50 years later, and it's way better than 20/20. I remember reading a study by a prominent psychologist who was trying to understand how Hitler came into power. His ultimate conclusion was that the Germans had centuries of indoctrination of obedience and discipline, and they were ripe for the taking. They would follow whatever made them feel strong. This tendency was often the desire of madmen, which is why the Romans called them Barbarians. I know this is a complete oversimplification, but that's the mindset I had during World War II, as I was getting pushed around. I thought then, and I think now, that the best way to understand your enemies is to know them.

We never really knew the depth of World War II as it went on. A war is a war, and people get killed, but it wasn't until we saw the newsreels in the theaters that broadcast the holocaust and the gas chambers that it really added up. I can remember friends of mine going to the show to have a good time and then running into the lobby to vomit after they'd seen footage of the atrocities. It was absolutely insane.

I took this same vengeance into the classroom and interrupted proceedings on a regular basis. One day, I got a note that I had to go the principal's office. I knew that I already held the Philadelphia high school record for getting expelled and re-instated. I think I refined that art. This time I was not expecting anything, so it threw me off. To make matters worse, our principal was Clarence Williams, a highly respected, former pro-football player.

Mr. Williams was cordial and confronted me on my outbursts in history class. I stated my feelings as eloquently as I could, but I still fully expected to be punished. Instead, he agreed with me! I was in shock, but when he gave me that opening, I was sure to make mention that I thought Shakespeare was anti-Semitic. Charles Dickens seemed fond of making fun of Jews, and I couldn't appreciate how great their work was when I knew deep down inside they hated my people. I felt compelled to make these statements. Principal Williams confided in me that he would tell my teachers to lighten up and not try to mold me.

"Harvey," he said, "We are expected to mark everyone with this "another good American" stamp as they leave this school. I'm learning that we can be good Americans and be Jewish, Black, Irish, Italian, German, or English, but it's more important to just to be good. We're all Americans because we live here together."

I couldn't believe my ears. He was speaking the truth as clearly as I'd every heard it. The principal got it! I could feel the tension in the room completely dissipate. I felt like I had a really solid new friend. As the conversation wound down, he was even more cordial. Then, he let me in on the real reason why he'd called me into his office.

"Harvey," he confided, "I have a very important dinner with some prospective clients tonight, and I really want this meeting to go well."

"How can I help?" I asked.

"Harvey," he said sheepishly, "I have never been to a Jewish home in my life, and I have no idea what to do. This meeting is really important to me, and it has to go well."

I got up from my seat, walked behind his desk, and leaned over. Immediately, he recognized that we were in a huddle, and I whispered out my instructions. He took them just as if I was going to hand him the ball and he was to run up the field for a touchdown. As we stayed in the same, hunched-over position, I imparted him with a ton of Jewish wisdom I thought he would need for that evening's get-together. His

The Bunny Hop

secretary barged in, and it was a bit embarrassing, as I pretended to be the quarterback and made handoff after handoff, while he pretended to take off running each time. Hey, it was serious male bonding.

Principal Williams got his deal, and I got my clearance in class. I could be as obstinate as I wanted, and they let me have my say. As long as I turned my work in on time, I was okay. If they wanted us to write a book report, I'd pick a book on a great Jew that was not on the list of preferred reading, and that was that. It made me incredibly proud that I was being accepted, and my confidence grew. I was ready to make some big moves.

I started with producing my own Bar Mitzvah. I got the blessing from my parents. Hell, I was saving them a ton of work. I wanted things to go my way, and planning it was a great experience. First off, there was no way I was going to use the regular house band at the Synagogue. The drummer looked like he belonged in a home for the aged, and the piano player was a number one candidate for a heart attack, so I wanted to liven things up. I picked my own all-star band. There were no Sunday shows in those days, so I found a lot of good musicians with that day off, and then I built a killer ten-piece band thanks to Bobby Roberts. I wanted a woman to sing the religious songs, not a male Cantor. That was unheard of in that day, but I did my homework and found a female Cantor!

My friends took all of the good spots at the head table; my relatives had to sit further back. I promoted this celebration as an act of compromise, because I was going against strict Orthodox tradition. We still had a Rabbi make sure the food was kosher and to bless the occasion, even if everything was unorthodox!

We had a feast. I did not want chicken, so I ordered roast beef. My band rocked the room, and we tore up the dance floor during jitterbug dance style numbers while that female Cantor really let her hair down. The way I looked at it, if I was now a man, which is the reason for Bar Mitzvahs, then I could run the show. I'm sure I offended more than a few people, but I bet I won a whole bunch more over to my side when they had a great time. I must have been right, because I earned a king's ransom; I scored some real nice *gelt* that day!

As much as I make light of it, I am very proud to be Jewish. Hey, who wouldn't want to known as "chosen?" In 1948, I won a national essay contest, and my letter was sent to the first president, Chaim Weitzman, of the brand new country of Israel. His first order of business on his initial day in office was to answer my letter. His reply hung for years in a frame on the wall of the Temple Shalom in Philadelphia, where I was Bar Mitzvah'd.

UNCLE GENE

My father was a big music fan, and he bought a lot of records. My mother was pretty talented, too, and had been quite a dancer when she was young. My grandmother was a big fan of the theater, burlesque, musicals, and movies. Being surrounded by all this, I gravitated mostly towards music. I first started picking out music I liked by about the time I was five years old. I started buying records when I was really young, and I had a huge collection early. I had an insatiable appetite for music. I liked a wide variety of artists, and was willing to play anything. I could listen to records all day if I didn't have this one thing that kept getting in my way; school.

As I evolved as a music fan, I was particularly fond of the big band era. My favorite was Benny Goodman when he had Gene Krupa on drums. The first time I saw the Benny Goodman Big Band with Gene Krupa, I was in the second grade. The show was at the Earl Theater at 8th and Market Streets. I cut school that day to get in line early, so I could get close to the stage. Once in line, I saw my elementary school teacher in line, as well. We made a deal: He wouldn't turn me in for ditching school, and I wouldn't snitch on him because he called in sick.

It was like that in those days. The parents and the kids liked the same music. We didn't have the famous "generation gap" that we do now, and it wasn't until rock and roll came along that, musically, the sons and daughters would leave their parents' music behind.

There were signs that the kids of that day wanted to break out. I think it started with the slang. It gave my mother fits, because she took everything I said literally until she caught on. I'd tell her I was going to "split," and she thought I ripped my pants. If I told her I had a "gas," she thought I was talking about flatulence. Later, when I got interested in girls, I would call a gal like Rita Hayworth a "mouse." She'd say, "We need to call the exterminator?"

I called Kim Novak a "gasser" once, and my mother thought I personally knew that she farted a lot. It was a way of saying that Kim had all the necessary body parts. If I said someone was "loose," it meant she knocked me off my tracks, but if I called a girl a "poppin," that meant she had all the bases covered. She was a "gasser," who made me "loose," and I was really "poppin." I don't think my mother ever took it all in, but she tried.

That Benny Goodman show was incredible, and Gene Krupa was amazing. I was completely in shock when I saw him live. He was so loud, so visual, and so incredibly great. I felt like I was getting thumped in the chest every time he hit his drum set. To me, he was the ultimate musician. He just overpowered his instrument. He could do anything with his kit, and I became a huge fan of his. I also knew right then, at the age of seven, that music was my calling. I wanted to dive into that world headfirst.

I bought every Benny Goodman record there was, and anything Gene Krupa played on. When those two were on the same stage there was no other band that could rock and swing like they could. They just tore the place up. Sometimes I had to buy those records twice, because I wore my first copy out. I was fascinated by Gene Krupa, and I still am. In 1945, after I saw a concert starring a great sax player from Philly, Charlie Ventura, I got to meet my idol. I can still remember it like it was yesterday. I was only nine years old, and to me, he was the greatest performer I had yet seen. He was really nice to me, and I had no problem telling him how great I thought he was. Surprisingly, he took me into his confidence. We just sat there talking like regular guys, even though I was just a kid. I thanked him for his time, and told him I wanted to stay in touch. We did. Every time Gene would come into town, I would go by to see him. He always remembered me, and we would spend time together. As I grew older, I would drive out of town to see his shows, and he would come over to Philly a lot because it was such an easy trip from New York, where he lived. He asked me if I wanted to play on his softball team. I jumped at the chance, and played on his famous team for seven years, even if I had to be the catcher! We'd often just linger about after the game, shooting the breeze. That's where he influenced my life forever.

I asked him about his prison term, and he was honest with me. What got him in real trouble was his independence. He always wanted to break out on his own. The cops planted marijuana in his bag, trumped up the charges, and sent him up the river. He was acquitted, but they stole six months of his life while he was in his prime. The cops were the real criminals in that scenario. That didn't break him; it just made him stronger and made him bitter. I told him how our family got ostracized by some anti-Semitic Philly cops just because we were Jewish, and he told me he understood. He would go on and on about how bad cops had gone out of their way over the years to get rid of hot, threatening new talent like Louis Armstrong, Eddie Cantor, himself, and others. He wanted no part of that life again, and gave it to me straight.

The big band leaders in those days were like drill sergeants. They ran their outfits like they were commanding the Army. There were very strict rules: No smoking, no drinking, be on time, dress great, and play your ass off. He said there were days that Benny made the band play a song a hundred times, until he felt they got it right. There were no drugs in the Big Band scene, and everybody knew that. In New York, you had to be a member of the musicians union or you couldn't play live. If you had a drug bust on your record you couldn't work in the city. The big bands provided steady employment for the best musicians, so nobody wanted to fall off the wagon and lose that weekly paycheck. It was a lot better way to make a living than jumping from gig to gig and wondering where you'd be playing each week and when you'd get paid. The risk was too high. That's why it looked so stupid when they set-up Gene with marijuana. He never used the stuff. If anybody was smoking "reefer" in those days, it would have been those in the bop groups who were on their own or in small combos, because you could not get away with that kind of behavior if you were working for Glenn Miller, Tommy Dorsey, Benny Goodman, or any of them. It was a very competitive time, artistically, and the leaders of the Big Bands kept their musicians in training.

Because of Gene's advice I will never drink, even for religious ceremonies, and I have never ever taken any drugs in my life. First off, I'm not interested, and why would you want to give the corrupt cops I knew any help? I like to joke that Jews make lousy alcoholics. After all, we make Manischewitz, the worst wine in the world, and how much fun could it be as a *shikker* drinking that *pishechtz* all day long?

I was happy to see Gene got the best arrangers when he struck out on his own, including Gerry Mulligan, Ed Finkel, and George Wallington. He always kept in touch and often would invite me to the band's rehearsals in New York, where I could see how the band put the show together. Watching some of the greatest musicians in the world working out all the kinks was a fascinating experience. It was invaluable lesson I took advantage of when I would build my own big band years later. Because I knew Gene, I was allowed to tag along. I got into the Steel Pier in Atlantic City for free, and I saw all the great big bands. That was a great place where I think I saw them all: Ray Anthony, Les Brown, Louis Bellson, Tommy Dorsey, Jimmy Dorsey, Benny Goodman, Gene Krupa, Stan Kenton, Kay Kyser, Spike Jones, Tex-Beneke, Glenn Miller, Ralph Flanagan, Charlie Barnett, Vaughan Monroe, Charlie Spivak, Sammy Kaye, Glen Gray and Casa Loma Band, Buddy Morrow, and Woody Herman. I thought that scene would go on forever, but in my mind, the musicians' strike did in the whole scene. It was a lot like the baseball strike in 1994, when they lost the World Series. The fans felt left out. Why couldn't the musicians and those they were fighting do battle behind closed doors and keep on playing?

Gene Krupa was a hall of fame musician and a hall of fame guy to me. When I look back at my childhood, I find it ironic how much advice about life I took to heart from such odd places outside of my family.

JUDI

As a family, we weren't very good Jews by definition. You could only get us in Temple for the high holy days. There was no way we would ever be Orthodox Jews. Honestly, that would have taken too much time for four people pulling in four different directions. I certainly knew I was not going to be Orthodox in anything. I did, however, attend Hebrew school as I was growing up, and I became quite fond of the Beth Shalom that Andrew Lloyd Wright designed in Elkins Park.

One Sunday, a friend invited me to a Bar Mitzvah. I was reluctant to attend. I would have preferred to go into town to look for new records, but once I was convinced it would be a good time, I decided to tag along.

My life was changed forever. As I entered the room it was as if someone had tugged my head around so I could see her. I stared so unashamedly, because across the room was the most beautiful woman I had ever laid eyes on. I had to meet her. As the ceremony went on, all I could think of was the strategy I would use to introduce myself. Here I was, fearless on stage, but after I saw her, my knees were worthless. I could hardly stand up. When the band started playing, I thought for sure I could ask her to dance, because with all of the dancing lessons I had, I would surely make an impression. What I forgot to realize was that the other boys in the room had eyes as big as mine. They all saw how beautiful she was, too. She must have danced with five other guys before I butted in and got my turn. Maybe I was dreaming too much, but I had a feeling that she wanted to dance with me too.

The Bunny Hop

I quickly introduced myself and learned her name was Judi Norvick. Now that I was right where I wanted to be, I wouldn't let anyone else cut in. I was determined to dance until the very end with her and hopefully get her phone number, or maybe even walk her home. We danced to "You Belong To Me," "Unchained Melody," "With These Hands," and "Perfida." It was bliss.

When the band announced the last song, I bravely asked if I could drive her home. To my great relief, she said yes! I did have one problem, I had come to the party with a friend and didn't have my car, so I quickly promised another friend a huge favor if he would let me borrow his car and give Judi a ride home. Fortunately, he said yes, and we made all the arrangements in about thirty seconds. There was one predicament I didn't like: I had to take my sister home, too.

Judi and I walked into the parking lot hand in hand, and my little sister was giggling behind us. I was savoring every moment with Judi, and I drove the long way to her house, going as slowly as I could. I stole a couple of kisses at stop signs and red lights, while my sister laughed hysterically in the back seat. When we finally got to Judi's house, I asked for her phone number and promised I'd call her as soon as I could.

I called her as soon as I got home to make sure the number worked; I wasn't going to wait for fate. Instead, I was going to bribe the jury. Judi was a real gem. She had brown hair, green eyes, a luscious smile that could melt your heart, and she was built to go! She was only fourteen, and I was sixteen but I felt like I had already met the girl of my dreams.

Judi lived in the Oak Lane section of Philly and came from a successful middle class family. I spoke often with her mother when I called over and got a feeling that she was smart, protective, and disciplined. She limited our calls at first but never budged on one front. When I asked Judi out for our first date, I was informed, much to my chagrin, that Judi was allowed to go out once a week. I tried to maneuver my way around this roadblock by driving over to Olney High, where Judi went, and hoping I could spot her and give her a ride home.

My father bought me a green 1952 Chevy when I turned 16. It was my pride and joy. Any time I could get Judi into my car for a date, I felt like the most important guy in the world. I wasted no time, and spared no expense. I was going to show Judi the good life. Since I had wheels, we could go anywhere. I was determined not to do the normal dinner and movie routine, because I wanted us to see and experience so much more. We went to nightclubs, great restaurants, and Broadway plays. We visited the Academy of Music to hear Eugene Ormandy's Philadelphia Pop Orchestra; the sky was the limit. My father gave me a very generous allowance that was more than a lot of fathers brought home as a paycheck. My mother and my grandmother never wanted me to work. They wanted me to go to college and get an education. I remember taking an aptitude test when I was young. My parents hoped the results would suggest that I would have the innate abilities to be a doctor, lawyer, or at worst, an accountant. Instead I was told that I'd be best suited as a Rabbi! I knew right then that those tests were suspect. If they were accurate, they would have suggested that I would become a comedian or a big band leader.

Judi and I had a routine I honored faithfully. I would shower, shave, find some great cologne and wear a different outfit every time I could. I'd pick her up at 7:00PM sharp and we would hit the town. I took her to the Latin Casino, the Celebrity Room, and Palumbo's. We saw Sammy Davis, Jr., Joey Bishop, Buddy Greco, and Don Rickles in those rooms. Whenever a big band came to town, we'd always make sure to catch Benny Goodman, Tommy Dorsey and Elliot Lawrence with their bands. It was such an exciting time, and I felt like I was right in the midst of this most important era in music.

Philadelphia had more nightclubs and places to see music than any other city in America, so naturally, many more artists came to Philly than anywhere else. With Judi, I got to enjoy so much of that time in the first few rows.

Some nights, we just wanted to have a romantic, leisurely dinner and enjoy the ambiance. Our favorites were Johnny Saxin's Original Bookbinder's, the Warwick Hotel, and Phillip's Italian Restaurant, which featured exquisite Sicilian cuisine on the corner of Broad and Ellsworth in South Philly. Then there was Ralph's, which was the oldest Italian restaurant in America. Legend has it that this was the first place where tomatoes were used in Sicilian cooking. A Jewish doctor came to the conclusion that tomatoes were not poisonous, and he encouraged the Italians to incorporate them in their recipes. It was a very small place that was well-lit and over two-hundred years old. It didn't have much of an atmosphere, but the food was incredible. Another Italian place we loved was Popi's. It was in South Philly on the corner of 20th Street and Passyyunk. We couldn't go there very often, because it was extremely elegant and expensive. I would order veal parmegiana and spaghetti for two, and with no drinks, the bill would come to $30.00. By 1952 standards, that was a small fortune. Every detail in this wonderful Italian establishment was paid attention. The décor and acoustics were so good that you couldn't hear who was talking in the booth next to you. Everyone could enjoy the arias of the great Italian singers the restaurant played through a fine sound system. The ambiance was romantic and softly lit. The service was outstanding. The waiters would always offer a light to those who wanted to smoke. Once I made my breakthrough, I never waited for a table, even if there was a long line. The food was divine. They imported many of their ingredients directly from Italy, and I never tasted veal that was as good as it was at Popi's.

Because the place was so discreet and had fabulous food, it was quite popular. All of the show biz types would hang out there after hours. It was a very elite place, and because it was so big, it could accommodate quite a crowd. Everybody knew it was where the Mafia went to eat.

Jack Guisard's Steak House wasn't famous for nothing. One of their specialties was aged prime rib of beef, and, over two inches thick, it was pure pleasure. In any of these fine establishments you could order blindfolded and still be sure to get a fine meal. Thanks to our speedy metabolisms as teenagers, we never gained a pound.

On nights we were feeling more adventurous, we would drive across the Delaware River and into New Jersey to dine at Cinnelli's, another fine Sicilian restaurant, or at Chubby's, The Hawaiian Cottage, or Stanley Schwarts' Black Angus. Often, we'd make it a foursome because my best friend, Clay Cohen, was going with Judi's best friend at the time. Those dinners were some of the best fun any teenager could ever have. I started to feel my oats after a few dates, and one night I put a nickel in a "soundie" to play one of my favorite songs. I bragged to Judi, "One day you're going to have to pay to hear my music."

She came right back with, "One day you're going to have to pay for the pleasure of my company."

I got her back good. "That should be a problem?"

I treated those dates like a personal challenge to better each one, and if I couldn't, I would think of something that was different, but every bit as special. Judi and I were in love, and I couldn't try any harder than I did. I sensed Judi's mother was getting a little concerned when she mentioned one restaurant was too expensive and Judi blurted out, "Harvey and I go there all the time!"

PHILLY'S THE PLACE

    In 1952, Philadelphia was the capital of the music universe. More records were being sold there than any other city in America. More than New York, Chicago, or Los Angeles, despite the fact that our population lagged behind New York and Chicago, and that L.A. had Hollywood. I think there were several reasons why. We had great record stores all over town. There was The Jazz Shop downtown, where they carried the finest selection of jazz records anywhere. You could find anything there. Krantz's on Broad Street in South Philly had a real hometown feel. They carried all the Mummers records. They specialized in local artists and made a concerted effort to be faithful to the talent of Philly by promoting their records in their hometown. Quite often, the actual artists would come into the shop themselves to look at their own records in the racks and to shoot the breeze with the customers and the owner. Sobell's in Oxford Circle and Bond's in Frankford specialized in the current hits and had sound booths where you could go and listen to the records before you decided if you wanted to buy them. It was a great place to spend an afternoon.
    I liked going to the "Black record stores" for a number of reasons. First off, they carried some great music you could only find there, and the owners knew everything about the records. The three main shops in Philly were the Paramount Record Shop on 16th and South Street, Milt's on 23rd and South Street, both in south Philly, and the Blue Note Record Shop at Ridge and Columbia in North Philly. Paramount's was my favorite. It was the largest and most popular of the three stores, but

The Bunny Hop

I learned some great lessons about life inside those walls.

I first noticed the store when I was on a shopping trip with my parents when I was twelve. The owner had put speakers out on the sidewalk so the passersby could hear what was being played inside the store. It was some of the most incredible music I had ever heard in my life. I walked into the store while my parents went into another shop, nearby. I used to be really good at wandering away like that; sometimes I had to do it in order to entertain myself. Once I walked inside the store I noticed that everyone was Black. I could see that a couple of people were looking at me funny. One of them said, "Little boy, you must be lost."

"No Ma'am," I said, "I know right where I am going." I kept walking right to the counter and looked up at the owner and operator of the store who also had a funny look on his face for me. He'd never had any small White kids as customers. He was really polite and said, "May I help you, son?"

"Sure," I said, "This music is great. What is it?"

I knew a bit about the music the Black crowd enjoyed, but what I heard that day was really different. Sure, I'd heard the mainstream artists like Nat King Cole, the Mills Brothers, Lena Horne, and Duke Ellington, but I had bought those records at the regular pop record stores. This was a deluxe specialty store that opened my eyes and ears to a whole new world. I was dying to find out what he was playing.

"It's Billy Ekstine," he said. "Save up enough money and you can buy it."

"I have enough money to buy it now."

His name was Felix Valgara, and he played so much other music I had never heard, including Dinah Washington, Sarah Vaughan, Dizzy Gillespie, and Count Basie.

I thanked him and started looking through the racks for a couple of artists I was curious about. I asked if they carried any Charlie Christian; that took them by surprise. I was mingling with the customers pretty well, and got friendly with a couple. I started "scatting" a song I'd heard on the radio. A lady in the store recognized it right away, and took me over to the Ella Fitzgerald section. Along with four records under my arm, I had the attention of the whole store. One of the old ladies in the store remarked, "The little White boy must have some

Black blood in him."

I heard her and felt compelled to answer her back. "I'm Jewish, but Jews and Blacks work great together as musicians." Then, I started to try and build up some points.

"You know," I said, "Lena Horne married big time Hollywood music arranger Lonnie Hayton, and Pearl Bailey married Louie Bellson, both of whom are Jewish. And if we go way back, King David married Beth Sheba, so you might have Jewish blood in you and I might have some Black blood in me!" I walked up to the counter and I made my first purchase. Then I asked him, "If I continue to be a customer of yours will you tell me everything you know about this music?" He laughed and said, "Sure but that will take years!" The whole store heard him and cracked up. "I've got lots of time, I'm only twelve!" By now everybody in the store was really nice to me, and I had a bunch of new friends. One old lady just shouted out, "Praise the Lord! If only all White boys would be like this!" I took my cue. I started doing the Nicholas Brothers' (a very popular Black dance team) strut and started singing "Drinkin' Wine (Spottie Ottie)" by Sticks McGee. I got an escort to the door as about a dozen people started dancing and singing along with me. It was a magical moment. When we got outside the store, my parents just froze when they saw me surrounded by a crowd of dancing and singing Black Americans. I had a blast.

When I waved good-bye and walked across the street to rejoin my parents, my father asked me, "What the hell was that all about?"

"I was just hanging out."

All he could say was, "Harvey, you got some *chutzpeh*!"

I like to think I got my street Ph.D. in Black music history inside that store. They turned me on to all the great artists of the 30's and 40's. Years later, when I got a radio job on WHAT 1340AM, which was a Black radio station at the time, Paramount's was one of my first sponsors. I am totally indebted to Felix at Paramount's for all the knowledge and love of music he shared with me. When I got old enough, he also told me where all the great music clubs were.

There were more nightclubs from Philly down to the New Jersey shoreline than in any other area of the country. In Philadelphia, our favorite nightspots were Ciro's, the Latin Casino, Palumbo's, and the Celebrity Room. Down the turnpike in Atlantic City, which was only a short forty-five minute drive away, were the 500 Club, the Presidential, and The Cotton Club. The Presidential Club was the home of the big Mambo revolution that was sweeping the nation, and it regularly featured Tito Puente, Niro Morales, Tito Rodriguez, and Neil Lewis. It was a great place to dance and learn all the new steps, and it had a very friendly crowd that welcomed everyone. The Cotton Club, since immortalized in film, featured only Black artists, or as they were called in those days, "race" acts. However, they would take anybody's money that wanted to go down to the clubs and hear some great music. I remember seeing Sammy Davis, Jr., the Will Masten Trio, the Nicolas Brothers, Al Hibler, and Billy Ekstine there.

Philly has always been in the shadow of New York City, and a lot of people preferred to go to the Big Apple for their entertainment. If you wanted to drive ninety minutes or catch a train into the big Apple, there were Broadway and all the great theaters. But in Philly, we had our own great theaters. At the Schubert, Erlanger, Walnut Theater, Keith, and Mastbaum theaters, you could see Broadway musicals and shows before they went to New York. Most of the shows that made it to Broadway started out in Philly. Often they were being developed and refined but took their form in the City of Brotherly Love before they hit the Big Apple. These shows had to make it in Philly just to get to New York, and we knew that. The big bands played at the Earl Theater, and there was no other place as grand. It was a big, stylish theater with a Moorish look to it. It had thick red carpeting, huge drapes, and classy chandeliers. The balcony was beautiful, and you had to walk up this big, carpeted staircase to get there. Whenever you had a ticket to the Earl to see a big band, you had to be dressed up! All the gentlemen wore sports jackets or suits, and all of the men wore ties! I never saw anybody go to that beautiful theater in khakis. I can remember those shows like it was yesterday; they had so much style. First up on the evening's bill for the show which cost all of a quarter, would be a first run movie. Then, when the film was over, the screen would go up, and slowly the stage would rise, exposing a great big band. They'd already be playing their signature song, and in no time, the aisles would be full of people dancing and swinging to their hearts' content. The band would play hit after hit and, in the middle of their set, would usually bring out the featured vocalist. The bands' sets were mainly instrumentals, and the musicianship was unmatched. Those cats could *play*, and their solos were to die for. I went as often as I could.

If you wanted to hear the symphony, there was no better place than the Academy Of Music. A lot of folks would drive the twenty-five miles out of town to the Sunnybrook Ballroom outside of Philly, in Pottstown, to see big bands that were on tour. If you just wanted to walk through the streets and see what was up, there were neighborhood lounges everyplace, where torch singers would play three sets a night, or little jazz combos would be playing nightly and trying to build up a following. There were so many of these little clubs, that a new band could literally "tour" Philadelphia. They could do this one week in one area of town, and then move to another section for another run. until they had played as many as a dozen of these rooms and reached almost everybody who lived in Philadelphia. There were just so many places musicians could play that Philly became a magnet for artists, and so encouraged its own talent to emerge. Plus, the music and entertainment never stopped. All over town there were "after hours" and "private clubs" where you had to be a member to attend, but these gatherings had special licenses that allowed them to serve alcohol until 4:00AM, while the rest of the town had to shut down liquor sales by midnight. So, if you didn't want the evening to end after seeing a great show, all you had to do was make the right connections, and you could finish off the evening by seeing Redd Foxx or Don Rickles tearing those rooms up. Both Foxx and Rickles were huge favorites in those clubs before they ever crossed over to the mainstream audience and before their recordings came out from behind the counter and into the regular bins. There were so many great places to play, and so many great artists performing, that A&R guys and talent scouts from the record companies had to hang around to see who was worthy of a brand new recording contract.

But what set Philly ahead of every other metropolis of that era were the great radio stations. Music wasn't broadcast twenty four hours a day on radio like it is now. Instead, the stations were programmed so you would have to tune in at specific times to listen to your favorite style of music, DJs or personalities. I was one of the first ones to own a big Emerson radio, a deep red, portable model that was extremely powerful. I could pick up every station in town, and at night, I could

The Bunny Hop

zero in on stations from New York, Detroit, and as far away as Chicago! I was a huge fan. I practically built my life and schedule around my favorite radio shows of that era. WIBG 990AM had Doug Arthur's "Danceland" on the air from 10:00AM until Noon, and then came back on again from 4:00PM to 7:00PM. WPEN 950AM had the talented Ed Hurst and Joe Grady locked in from 2:30PM to 6:00PM. At night, kids would tune into the Black jocks like Georgie Woods, who broadcast on WHAT 1340AM from 9:00PM till Midnight, or Jacko Henderson who could be heard on WDAS 1400AM during the same time slot.

The favorite station for the mainstream audience was WPEN 950AM, where you could hear Pancho play Mambo music from 9:00PM to 11:00PM. Or, if you preferred, you could go down to the studio and dance to the great Latin music he played. Later, Eddie Newman had a popular show called "Open House," which ran from 3:00PM to 6:00PM on WDAS. If you had a powerful receiver, there was the "Make Believe Ballroom" show hosted by Martin Block on WNEW that aired from 10:00AM to Noon and from 4:00PM until 6:00PM. Philly also had an all night radio show called Dawn Patrol with Joe McCalley, who was an institution. Back in those days, you couldn't call into the station to request songs. The only way to reach Joe was by Western Union. You literally had to send a telegram to get your favorite song played on the air.

My favorite show, without question, was Bob Horn's Bandstand, which was broadcast on WFIL 560AM. Bob had an easygoing style and low-key demeanor. He was the kind of guy that could make anybody comfortable, and he loved all kinds of music. He was a tremendous innovator, and many of his original ideas are common staples in the entertainment business today. We first heard him in Philly as a DJ. Originally, he was a salesman and a real hustler who was quite successful at what he did, but it was soon apparent that he knew more about music than all the DJs around, so they put him on the air. He was a huge hit. Bob had this deep affection for Jazz and Rhythm & Blues that went well beyond the boundaries of the regular pop music of the era. He had a keen ear for talent and introduced so many of us to the great, breaking new talents of the day. I can still remember leaning up next to my deluxe Emerson where I heard some great new music for the first time, courtesy of Bob Horn. The core artists that made up his presentation were Billy Eckstine, Dizzy Gillespie, Duke Ellington, Louis Armstrong, the Mills Brothers, Nat King Cole, Errol Graner, Louis Jordan, Sammy Davis Jr., Sarah Vaughan, Ella Fitzgerald, and Cab Calloway. Philadelphia was definitely the center of America's popular music scene. The number of talented artists that hailed from in and around Philly through those early years is staggering. The list includes Buddy Greco, Buddy Defranco, Nelson Eddy, Jeanette MacDonald, Gerry Mulligan, Stan Getz, Red Rodney, Pearl Bailey, Bill Haley, the Four Aces, Joey Bishop, Eddie Fisher, Charlie Ventura, Lillian Roth, Frankie Avalon, Chubby Checker, Gloria Mann, Kitty Kallen, Mario Lanza, Bobby Rydell, Leroy Lovett, Ethel Waters, Solomon Burke, Dinah Washington, the Nicholas Brothers, Ernie Kovas, Dick Lee, Georgie Shaw, Danny & The Juniors, Irving Berlin, Len Barry, Danny Kaye, and Lee Morgan.

Bob Horn's Bandstand became a staple on WFIL's schedule, and whatever time they put the show on the air it just kept growing. Bob was becoming a celebrity and was very well-respected by his audience and those in the industry, even the executives that would fight his every move for his whole career. They admonished him not to play "race" records, those made by Black musicians and which were previously only played on Black radio stations. Horn refused and had a policy that any great music could find a home on Bandstand, no matter who was the creator. At that time in Philly, Bob had the Midas touch and everybody knew it. WFIL got a television license and began broadcasting regularly in the late forties. In 1952, they finally approached Bob Horn to do a TV show. At first he was reluctant, thinking it would take away from his popular radio show. When they asked him to do both, he agreed. That would cement Philly's reputation as the hottest scene in the country.

The Bunny Hop

Bob Horn created Bandstand TV show in February 1952

BANDSTAND

It killed me that I couldn't see Judi on Friday nights, but I still had to get out into the evening. I've always been a night owl, and I've figured out how to go through life with just four to five hours of sleep a night. With school, social activities, Judi, and music, I had maybe five hours left to lie down and recover each day.

I loved radio, and I think most people that grew up in the thirties and forties felt the same way. Bob Horn was definitely my hero. I was dying to meet him, and, after I saw his picture in the newspapers a couple of times, I would look all around for him at nightclubs and restaurants hoping someday that I could walk up and introduce myself. That never happened, so one day I got really brave. I called information for WFIL's telephone number. Then, I dialed the station and waited nervously.

I expected to get rejected, because after all, I was just a high school junior, he was a major star in the town ready to explode, and there was a huge gap between us logistically. I was scared but so excited I had to measure my thoughts and remember what my grandfather, the doctor, had said years before: "Memorize your words before you say them." I hadn't stuttered in years, but if I was going to regress, this was the time.

"I'd like to speak with Bob Horn, please," I asked after his show was over.

"Speaking!" he said.

The Bunny Hop

Dimples and Harvey leading the kids on Bandstand,
to the Bunny Hop in 1952

"Hi Bob. My name is Harvey. I'm a big fan of yours, and I wanted to ask you a few questions. Do you have the time?"

"Actually I do. Harvey, how old are you?"

"Sixteen."

"Good; what do you like about the show?"

"Everything!"

"Thank you, but what would make the show better?"

"Less commercials… It seems like there are more commercials than music."

"Seems that way to me, too."

"Oh, I don't know. I think your show is perfect. I want to learn how to be a D.J."

"Harvey, be a student and fan of music. Learn the skills, and you can do what I do."

"No way, Mr. Horn. You're the best!"

"My name is Bob. Please call me Bob."

"Can I watch you to see how you do it?"

"Sure, someday. That would be fun."

"Well, Bob, thanks for your time. You've been really nice. Can I call you back?"

"Of course you can, Harvey, but tell me; what are the kids in the audience up to these days?"

"Well, most of the time they are hanging out at The Hot Shoppe, listening to the radio and dancing."

"Really? Where is that?"

"At Broad and Stenton on Friday nights, at about 9:00PM."

"Thanks for the tip, kid."

"Thank you, Bob."

The Hot Shoppe was a family style eatery that was founded in Washington, D.C. Then, they opened a new store in Philly in the forties, and it steadily grew in popularity. It was owned and operated by the same family that built the Marriott Hotel chain. In Philly it was a really popular restaurant where you could sit in your car and be served on trays that hung on your car door. We'd either do that, enjoying the evening air, or go inside the comfortable restaurant for dinner. The cuisine was pure Americana: Burgers, fries, shakes and cokes. So many people went there on dates, that it became a big hangout. Take your girlfriend out for dinner, and linger in the parking lot with your friends until it was time to go home. Everybody went there. I had many a meal there in my new Chevy.

Then, this phenomenon began to grow thanks to the radios in cars and the kids wanting to listen to fresh, new music. Within weeks, a ritual like no other grew to become the focal point of all Philly teenage nightlife. It started when one hot-shot with a new car ordered dinner and left the radio blasting in his car. Soon enough, a couple of other people came by to hear the great new songs on the radio courtesy of WFIL and Bob Horn. Slowly, this huge parking lot on the side of a restaurant became the best ever place in Philly to be on Friday night.

The guys would come with their new cars, park them at the edge of the lot, and all tune in to the same radio station. The dolls were soon to follow, dressed up and anxious. Soon enough, teenage Philly had an outdoor nightclub with no cover charge that played great tunes and had a crowd that overflowed. The owners of the restaurant didn't mind, rightfully. They thought it was good for business. The parking lot became one big dance floor where the kids would go wild.

In no time, The Hot Shoppe was the place to be and be seen. I had to look sharp. I took a cue from my father, who used to dress really nice. He was always shopping in the finest stores in town and bought most of his suits at an upscale shop called Diamond's on South Street. I picked up on his technique and wore the best clothes I could find. It was part of our family tradition. The men were expected to look good, as in successful, in order to become even more successful. At lot of my friends would kid me that I had over-dressed but I didn't mind, because that meant I looked sharp. If I was slipping, my mother would notice. She'd scream out, "You can't wear that *phakata* shirt! You might meet a nice, Jewish girl tonight. You need to look like a *mensch*!"

I liked the Ivy League look, which was more traditional and smart. I wasn't interested in getting a ducktail haircut or DA as it was called (short for duck's ass). I wanted to look razor-clean and smart. I didn't wear pleated pants; I wanted them pressed and unwrinkled, no cuffs thank you! I didn't wear the peg leg pants that were tight a round the ankle and rose three inches above your waist. I wore imported English shoes and kept them polished so they shone like a mirror. I wasn't into the rebellious attitude that was surfacing. I wanted to make a timeless fashion statement.

Watching what the kids wore could tell you which part of town they were from. The poorer kids had to stretch their clothing dollar, and frequented stores they could afford. The guys would go down to Arrow's or Snellenberg's on Market Street, or to Krass Brothers on South Street. The gals could go to the Fashion Bug or Mariann's, where there would be racks of cheaper dresses, blouses, and skirts. You had to be creative while shopping at the bargain stores, and mix up your wardrobe well. Any woman's nightmare was to show up at an important function with the exact same outfit as another coed. Some of the girls went with the bobby sox outfits, and I just hated that. It didn't look stylish at all. Once you were dressed right, it was time to go to the Hot Shoppe with your best buddies and have a great time. I loved going with my pals Clay Cohen, Gene Feldman, and Dave Brenner

Families would come by for dinner, and their teenage kids would ask to stay so they could dance and listen to the music. They'd beg for subway or bus fare home, as long as they could stay. By 9:00 PM the dance floor was sardine central. Everybody in Philly was dancing in the parking lot, or so it seemed. I made sure to be there every chance I could.

As the night wound down, it tended to get a bit competitive and often resembled the movies that showed the best couple getting singled out and surrounded by the other dancers, who admired the most accomplished dancers on the floor. I fought like an Olympic athlete to be inside that circle, and many a night I accomplished that goal. It was delicious fun, but Judi wasn't there. That started to concern me; I couldn't brag to Judi how I danced with another girl to win the crowd over. But I couldn't take her there, either. I wondered if I'd ever get to share everything with Judi, which is what I ultimately wanted to do. I was forced to live this double life because of her mother's restrictions.

I got brave and called Bob Horn more often. We became friendly, and I was dying to meet him. He would quiz me about what music the kids liked, and I'd beg him to be my mentor in the music business. I reminded him about The Hot Shoppe and told him the scene was exploding there.

Bob Horn's radio show, Bandstand, had been on the air for several years and was by far the most respected show in town. He expanded the hours, invented an adult version, and had now moved the show over to the new medium, television. The show was getting off the ground too slowly, and the station's management, which was always a thorn in Bob's side, thought the show was stagnating and might not make it. They tried all sorts of gimmicks to try and make the show better, but being suits and not entertainers their ideas usually stunk. If anyone was going to make the show better, it was going to be Bob.

"Mr. Horn, you have to see what's going on down at The Hot Shoppe. It is the coolest scene anywhere."

"If you say so, I'll have to go by. Give me directions."

I told Bob everything: Who, what, when, where, and why, and I reminded him not to be late!

I looked all over for Bob that night, but I never saw him. I missed more than a couple of steps, straining my neck to check out each car coming near the lot, but in the end I was convinced he hadn't come.

I was ashamed to call him the next week, thinking maybe he went by and didn't like what he saw.

What I didn't know was that he was blown away by what he saw, and he was in a position to create a very memorable moment in TV history. I was shocked one night when Bob called me to talk. Every time before, I had called him, but this time he called me. I still don't know how he got my number, but I was relieved and nervous to hear from him again. I sheepishly asked him if he went by The Hot Shoppe that night and he said he did, but it was so packed he could only walk around the perimeter of the gathering.

"I was looking all over for you, Bob; I wanted to introduce myself," I said, glad to be speaking with him again.

"I was looking for you too, Harvey, but the place was just so crowded. It did give me a great idea, and I'd like you to tell all your friends about it. We've decided to put teenagers on our show, dancing live to the hit records we are playing. I think it will liven up the show and be a lot of fun."

"Are you kidding?" I asked. "It will be the most fun ever,! Please tell me when and where."

Bob slowly explained his plans, and the word spread like wildfire. They even took out ads in the papers and posted signs inviting the teenagers of Philly to come down to the Bandstand set every weekday.

Harvey Sheldon and Dimples 1953 Jitterbugging

The Bunny Hop

Original Bandstand TV set. In 1952 Harvey Sheldon and Dimples, doing the Bunny Hop

It was like a teenage exodus to glory, or a hormonal pilgrimage to our new Mecca. Of course, I had to be first in line and showed up as early as I could.

The show would air live at 3:00PM everyday on WFIL, channel six, so that meant I had to get out of a class that ended at 2:30 PM by 2:20 PM to make it across town from Lincoln High School to the studios down on Broad Street. But make it I did.

The show was now complete, and it built a mold that was first invented by Bob Horn on WFIL, and copied a million times since. He would host the show from behind his little podium, give a short, concise little monologue to open the program, wherein he would mention the guests that would appear on the show, as well as contests and new records he'd be playing. The kids would be sitting in bleachers on the side of the dance floor while the show opened, but in no time we'd be out on the floor, cutting it up to our favorite new songs. That was a blast, but even more fun for me, being a huge music fan, was to see and meet some of the greatest artists of our time. Bob had a knack for picking out the best new talent, and the musicians were very appreciative and thankful for his support. He had a unique and special way he would introduce them. He would always say, "We've got company," and make us all feel like a great new star was walking into our living rooms.

Bandstand did feel like home to me. I spent almost every weekday afternoon there for over two years, and I saw some incredible artists, many of which I will be eternally grateful for and will never forget. In that time, Bob Horn's Bandstand had Nat "King" Cole, B.B. King, Al Hibler, and other brilliant artists of all styles.

I was very proud of the way Bob was "colorblind." Since he was such a huge fan of jazz, and so many jazz artists were Black, there was no way Bob would allow the dance floor to be lily white. Even on the very first shows, there were Black couples dancing on the floor along with white couples, and this was 1952 in Philadelphia. I don't think this could have happened in any other city. I can remember dancing with a beautiful Black gal in the early years and thinking nothing of it, but I'm sure it would have started a race riot in some more intolerant and ignorant city.

The show exploded, and I was beginning to feel my oats. I had a part in a Broadway show when I was a sophomore in high school, and I

The Bunny Hop

thought that was my ticket to fame. But, I got my walking papers after just two weeks. I was supposed to stick to the script, but every night I threw in a different joke. The audience loved me; the director canned my ass. When I went back to school, I was hoping to be a star, but I was put on a steady diet of humble pie for awhile by my friends. With Bandstand, I could feel I was backing a winner.

It seemed like everyone in town was either on Bandstand or at home watching Bandstand. One of the main sponsors of the show was Muntz, who was the leading retailer of televisions. Old Mad Man Muntz loved Bob Horn, because his show was forcing families to buy TVs by the thousands. Kids who lived in homes without TV sets made their parents miserable until they bought one, and when they did, the whole family loved the new addition to their home.

Pretty soon, I'd picked up the nickname "TV Harv," and I could hear people call me that all over town. It didn't hurt my image that I wore sunglasses nearly all the time, sometimes even at night. My eyes have always been super sensitive to light because of my genetic condition, but I have to admit I did it mostly for the looks.

One day, one of my best buddies played a prank on our family by making a bumper sticker that said "TV Harv" and slapping it on the bumper of my father's car. I thought my Dad would be mad about that, but he was actually quite amused and was proud of my newfound fame.

This notoriety didn't hurt my dates with Judi. Now, not only did I have the dough to go, I also had a face people recognized, which opened even more doors for me and Judi. I thought life could not get any better than this.

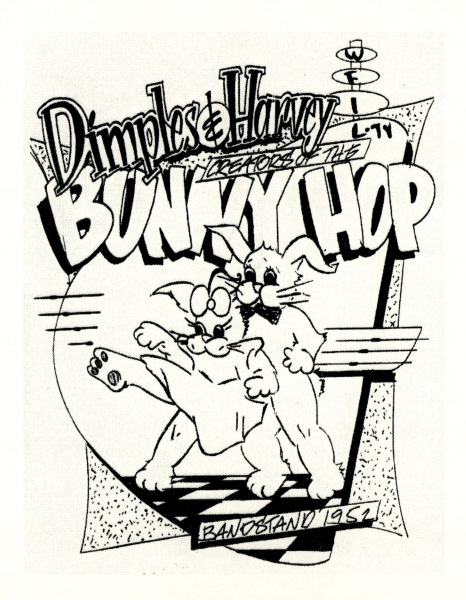

Dimples created the art work for a Bandstand TV-Bunny Hop T-Shirt

THE BUNNY HOP

On my trips to New York, I could see that the Big Apple ran far behind Philadelphia as a musical city. It was much more focused on plays, shows, and the past. I used to joke to friends that I thought New York was going to do the minuet forever. Philly was progressive and bountiful, and believe me, the record companies were well aware of that fact. Vinyl records just flew out of the stores in Philly during that time, and it seemed like everybody wanted a piece of that action. There were always record company promo men hanging around Bandstand, and when Bob got the TV version of Bandstand pumped up, his power and influence grew exponentially. The promo men's logical course of action was to get their records played on Bob Horn's Bandstand, and from there they could build a buzz that would spread all across the country and create a hit record. Radio was much more regional in those days, and the record companies took on regions one by one. Sometimes, it would take a full year for an artist to get his record played all the way across the country. But, if an artist got Bob Horn's blessing coming out of the box, that would be a huge first step. Remember, this was the infancy of pop radio promotion, and the record companies were just learning how to market their artists. Payola was a work in progress. Those promo moguls would wine and dine Bob Horn in their attempts to get their companies' records on his show, but he still had the integrity to back the artists he knew were really special. I watched many times how he supported artists he really believed in like Al Martino, Ray Anthony, Nat King Cole, Kate Starr, Tony Bennett, and Jerry Vale.

In a lot of ways, I think the record companies were first intimidated

The Bunny Hop

by Bob Horn's power, but they soon figured out a way to grease the wheel. I know they would have preferred to have the power Bob Horn had in-house, but that would look too obvious, so they played the game. I also saw similar scenarios, where a fresh, young radio promotion man would come in with a record that he was convinced was a smash. Bob would first put it on the show's rate a record segment, a skit Bob created. If the song got a low rating, it would be dead in the water.

The record business was rapidly changing. It was turning into much more of a business and a big money machine. The emphasis was shifting a bit more away from the pure joy of music, and toward the act of commerce and selling a product. The smaller labels, the equivalent of Mom and Pop stores, were being challenged by the new supermarkets, the major labels. At that time, the industry heavyweights were Columbia and Decca with Mercury Records and Capitol Records seeking their piece of the pie.

The Capitol Records team, being the newer kid on the block, was being more aggressive and creative. They were anxious to move up the food chain. One of their new talents was Ray Anthony, a former trumpeter from Glenn Miller's Big Band, who had struck out when he formed his own band. Ray was a very clever arranger and talented songwriter, but he was reduced to mainly doing cover songs, which can be seen as an insult to an artist who prides himself in original compositions. Ray had hits remaking "Can Anyone Explain" and the Ames Brothers "Sentimental Me." Ray Anthony had just recorded a new single for Capitol Records that had everyone at the label talking. A meeting of the minds at the company concluded that the song would have to be introduced on Bob Horn's Bandstand if it was to establish Anthony as a solo artist on his own merit.

By now, I was a regular on Bob Horn's groundbreaking and influential TV show. I'd gotten my picture in the newspaper on numerous occasions when the papers ran stories about Bob Horn. He loved being around kids, and usually, when they asked to take pictures of him on the set, he would ask the kids to crowd around so they could be in the picture, too. I had gone through several dancing partners on the show, but I met my match when I found Dimples.

THE BUNNY HOP

Harvey Sheldon and Dimples 1953
Flying High to the Bunny Hop

She was tall, blonde, and beautiful. Many said she looked a lot like Lauren Bacall. Like me, she had show-biz aspirations and hoped to take her talents to Broadway, as a dancer. We got along fine, and I made it clear that I had a steady girlfriend, but that didn't matter, because there was no way we could ever date. Dimples's boyfriend was the captain of the football team at Lincoln High, and I was spending all the time I could with Judi. Dimples lived in the Oxford Circle part of town, like I did, but we were worlds apart in other ways. Her father was a strict Baptist minister and had very strong conviction about how his daughter should behave. All we had in common were Bandstand and dancing. I liked it that way, because it was already awkward enough being seen on TV every day with one girl, and dating another on the weekends. Judi's mom never failed to make mention of that irony and was quick to point that out to her daughter. Dimples's boyfriend also rubbed in it pretty thick. I treated my relationship with Dimples as a business venture. I was helping her, and she was helping me. Together, we were viewed as the best dancers on the floor, and that was that.

One day, I remember seeing Artie Mogul from Capitol Records come by the studio to visit with Bob Horn. I'd seen him before, and I knew he was a big wig. I was hanging out after the show was finished, and we were winding down and sharing small talk before it was time to go home and hit the books. Artie, his associates, and Bob Horn disappeared into Bob's office for a few minutes, and shortly thereafter, I was approached by Julie Rosen, who was Bob Horn's long time secretary. Dimples and I were wanted in Bob's office. At first, I got really scared. What had I done to get admonished? I never tried any of my pranks on Bandstand. I was all business there. I couldn't for the life of me think of what we had done wrong. As we climbed up the stairs, Dimples and I both kept trying to figure out what we had done. When we entered Mr. Horn's office, he was sitting next to Artie and a couple of other local radio promo men and had a big smile on his face. That was very disarming.

"Harvey," Bob said, "This is Artie Mogul, and Artie, this is Dimples." He continued, "We have a new song that was just recorded by Ray Anthony that we are very proud of. We came here to play it first for Bob Horn, and he loves the song. We, at Capitol Records, are also convinced that the song will be a smash hit, but there's something missing."

THE BUNNY HOP

Jumping High in step to the Bunny HOP on Bandstand 1953

Dimples and I looked at each other. We still didn't know where these powerful people were going with this conversation.

"We need a dance to go along with the song, so we watched over the floor, and it was obvious to me and my friends here that you two were the best dancers on the floor."

I was blushing a little bit, even though I felt the same way.

"What we'd like to do is ask you two to create a dance to go along with the song, and we'll debut both of them on Bob's show on Friday afternoon."

I was in shock at first. I knew this was a huge opportunity, but what if we blew it? What if we invented a dance that was pathetic?

Before I could even collect my thoughts Dimples said, "We'd love to!"

"Then we've got a deal?" Artie asked, looking all around the room.

"Fine by me," Bob Horn said, and just like that, we were commissioned an opportunity of a lifetime.

Artie shook hands with everybody around and said he'd be back on Friday to bring in Ray Anthony to watch the show.. After a couple of minutes, it was just me, Dimples, and Bob Horn in the room. I thanked Bob profusely for the honor and the opportunity, but still expressed my concern.

"You kids will be fine," he said, handing us an advance acetate copy of Ray Anthony's new single with the words "Bunny Hop" handwritten on a white label.

Dimples jumped up and said, "We've got work to do."

We walked out of the studio that day sitting on a goldmine, but also under a very strict deadline. Dimples and I agreed to spend our lunch hour each of the next three days in the school's big community recreation room, where they had a turntable and we could try out different steps. At the time, the Congo line was creeping onto dance floors courtesy of the Latin musical influence, popularized by Tito Puente and the clubs that brought this innovative new style into town. However, it was more freeform and didn't represent any particular song. Instead, it adhered more to a certain beat. We wanted to come up with a simple step anybody could do, but which would also get everybody involved, like a Congo line does.

THE BUNNY HOP

Harvey Sheldon and Dimples in Sunday Today magazine section of the Philadelphia Inquirer cover March 1953.

The Bunny Hop

Dimples came up with the exact steps we were going to use, and I added my expertise as best I could. We decided that she would be in front and I would be behind, her holding her on her hips and following her every move in complete harmony. After two days we were good; by three days we were great and full of confidence. When Friday came, it was a relief that all the anticipation had finally evaporated, and now it was time to perform. I always thought that was the easy part. Thinking up good stuff does take work, but duplicating it when it's finished is a piece of cake.

Bob Horn stepped up to his podium just as he always did, and this time when he said, "We've got company," Ray Anthony walked on stage. After a brief little chat where Bob asked Ray about the song, he mimicked playing the song while they played the record over the P.A. That's what they did in those days. It was tough to get a band to sound right on TV, so most shows stuck to the singers' lip synching their songs. In this case, Ray pretended to blow his trumpet as he had in the studio when the song was recorded.

When the song began, Dimples and I were the only ones on the floor. We took one brief lap, demonstrating the steps. Then, all the kids joined in. Within a minute, everyone was in the groove, and the house was hopping. Dimples had a smile on her face that was worth a million bucks. When the song finished, the room exploded into cheers, and I think everybody knew the "Bunny Hop" was going to be a huge hit. I had one friend tell me that he was watching that show on TV, and the song was so infectious that he and his sister jumped up to do the dance. They hopped around just like they saw us do on TV, and when the song was over, they went back to hating each other just as they did before the song came on. Finally, the kids had a dance of their own. They didn't have to do just the foxtrot, the jitterbug, and all the dances their parents had handed down.

After the show, there were smiles all around. I felt like I must have shaken hands with people for over a half an hour. Artie Mogul was loving his new promotional idea and felt that now he could take it nationwide. I got a chance to meet Ray Anthony, whom I really admired, and wished him the best. It was the start of something great for Ray. After the "Bunny Hop" exploded and he had more big hits with "Dragnet" and "The Peter Gunn Theme," he would be taken very seriously as an original artist. He certainly does owe a lot of his success to Bob Horn's support.

My life and Dimples's life would change forever after that day. Each afternoon, we'd lead off the "Bunny Hop" on the show, as it became a featured favorite. The single sold 70,000 copies in three weeks in Philadelphia, more than any artist's ever, including Frank Sinatra's. Dimples's and my picture was on the cover of the song's sheet music tablature doing the Bunny Hop. That cover was sent to the Smithsonian Museum to preserve the piece of popular culture and its creation. Many of the local papers ran stories about the dance phenomenon, but when the Philadelphia Inquirer syndicated a three-page story in nearly every Sunday morning newspaper in America, it really hit me. The story closely documented the song's history, the dance craze, and it had diagrams showing the exact steps Dimples and I created. I was stunned at how fast all of this had happened, and I loved the spotlight. I felt like I'd finally become a *mensch*! I know Dimples enjoyed the adulation, too, but she was more humble about it than I was. Her boyfriend hated her success. Even though he was one of the best athletes in the whole city, his girlfriend was now more recognizable and famous than he was. He felt showed up, and I enjoyed watching him come unglued whenever I'd mention our success.

I was wondering how this was going to play out with Judi, though. She was mature beyond her years, but her mother had her ear. It made me a lot more comfortable when she congratulated me on my success and seemed to enjoy it as much as I did. I particularly enjoyed getting better tables at restaurants and being comped (paid for) occasionally. I did start to hear more and more remarks from Judi's mother that she felt Judi was missing out on the typical teenage years, but I didn't even think I was a teenager anymore. At least I wasn't acting like one, even if I was only sixteen. Her father dismissed our relationship as "puppy love," and said that we would both outgrow each other. I had a front row ticket to the high life, and I didn't see reason for Camelot to end.

HOME SWEET HOME

 At home, I never could understand where my mother and my father were going. Whenever they fought, I felt like I was being punished, and that it might be my fault. I cringed so many times when they screamed and yelled at each other. Then, there'd be nights when I didn't think there could be a more perfectly matched couple. They looked so happy together on the dance floor as they ate up the good life. I could tell they were getting prouder of me as I achieved more, and they even relaxed their anti-show biz stance a bit. But finally, the fighting came to a head. My mother took the house and car keys. She locked my father out of the house after a big fight, and would not open the door for him. He had to walk away with just the clothes on his back and find a place to sleep.

 The next morning, Mom had changed her tune and begged my father to come back. That went on for three straight days. She would follow him wherever she could, call him at work, and beg him to come back. Finally, he'd had enough of her volatility and said, "Never! You threw me out once, you'll do it again. Forget it. It's over!" My father filed the papers, and my mother refused to sign them.

 Divorce in those days was an unspeakable taboo. It was against every religion I knew, and it was quite an oddity to many Jews. I didn't know any other kids whose parents had divorced. I felt like a social leper and like people were staring at me and whispering behind my back. I could hear them in my mind saying, "There's Harvey, the kid from the divorced family." I had to hold my head up even though it was really hard to do.

With my father gone, it was just me, my sister, and my mother. Obviously, the big checkbook wasn't there anymore, so I had to figure out a way to fend for myself. My mother went to work, my sister quit school to go to work, and I was expected to give up my dreams and take the first job that came along. I refused and got a taste of the temper my mother used to reserve for my father. I told her I would be happy to contribute whatever I could to the cause, but I was not going to give up my life, even if she insisted.

As a young man, I still needed a father. I was pretty much full-grown physically, but emotionally, I still had a lot to learn from a patriarch. I tried calling him on several occasions, but I could never get him on the phone. It was like he completely disappeared.

I did bump into him at David Rosen Record Distributors, where we were both buying some new records. I was glad to see him, and I ran over to say hello, thinking we could re-establish our bond. I wanted to hug him and tell him how much I missed him, but he acted distant and reserved. What he told me that day were the harshest words I'd ever heard in my entire life, even if he thought he was being extraordinarily polite. He didn't even call me by my name. "I have a new family now, and you're not part of it."

"What?" I thought. "He's my father! I'm his son!" He walked away from me like he'd never seen me before in his life. He had remarried, and I was told by someone who knew him that his new wife had an even worse temper than my mother did. He was tortured later in life by diabetes, and had both legs amputated before he died. To this day, I have no idea where he is buried, so I can never pay my respects and say I'm sorry for anything I may have done.

After that day at the distributors, I was convinced that I would not hear from him, and I gave up trying.

I had to make due. I did what a lot of people do when they go through a huge personal loss. I completely buried myself in my work. That way, I would be too busy to feel the pain.

MY MAFIA FRIEND

I knew I couldn't do anything about my parents' break up. My best defense was to get out of the house and keep busy. I thought maybe my teenage years were causing their riffs, but in retrospect, how could I do that when I wasn't even there? The world was my oyster, and I wanted to be a shining pearl.

I was probably moving too fast. Those years felt like a roller coaster, and the worst part of any great ride is not getting on, it's getting off. It was so much fun condensed into too little time, but I am not complaining.

The most important friendship I made during those turbulent times was completely unexpected. I bumped into a fellow at a nightclub one night, when I shot off my mouth trying to get a few laughs. Everyone else was rather reserved, so I thought that opened up the stage for me. What I later learned was that the man who commanded the silence I abused was a Mafia boss, one of the most feared and respected men in Philly. Deeply entrenched in the underworld, Angelo Bruno had it all: Money, cars, guns and a powerful reputation. I naively thought he was a sucker for a good one-liner.

After telling a few jokes and watching him belly laugh so hard it could shake the tables, I thought I had a new customer. I was making friends with the scariest guy in the whole town. How was I to know? I was a fresh kid in high school trying to get into show business. To me, anywhere was a stage, whether it was a park bench, a bus stop, or a restaurant; no place was sacred. Well, actually I kept it clean in

The Bunny Hop

Synagogue (if they could get me in there). Honestly, it only takes one person to be an audience, and I worked any crowd I found as hard as I could.

I didn't know what the mafia was. I thought Mr. Bruno was a true gentleman. He had a suit on that was worth as much as a house. His watch would pull you under if you went swimming with it on. He wore the most expensive cologne. His nails were manicured. He certainly knew the good life; the man was impressive. After one of my more racy jokes told in a small circle of friends, he put his big mitts on my shoulder and took me aside.

"I like you kid," he said. "You tell the truth, which is what most people don't want to hear."

We kept talking, and I immediately felt comfortable with him.

He asked me what my plans were and where I was headed to in life, and I said, "To the top!"

He liked that, because he knew I had guts. When I walked back to my friends, they were really concerned that I was getting in too deep at too early of an age. Well, that was my modus operandi, anyway! They started to whisper to me who he was, and I just waved them off and called it a night.

Word traveled fast in those days, and I noticed more people liked me, but more kept a distance, which is what I wanted. If you are an entertainer, a "maybe" is just not going to cut it. People have to have an opinion. Your act has to work or you are off stage, and I wasn't afraid of the cruel truth. I just needed to know so I could get on with the show. I started to see Bruno everywhere as my social life evolved. We greeted each other with respect and always spoke of doing business together. He would make remarks that made me know I had a friend I could trust.

I went out to dinner with a bunch of friends one night, and we were having a grand old time being adults. We chatted up the waitress, got carded when we asked for drinks we knew we would never be served, and ate until we were ready to burst. When it came time to pay the bill, I had no wallet in my pocket. I turned my clothes inside and out looking for anything I could contribute to the tab, while I was getting redder by the second.

Suddenly, I felt that familiar, big paw on my shoulder. It was

Angelo, who just happened to be sitting in another booth across the room and witnessing my ordeal.

"Good to see you, Harvey," he said. "Come on over to my table. I want you to meet my friends, and they want to hear your proposition about tomatoes."

Of course, I jumped at the chance. What other choices did I have, other than washing dishes at the restaurant for a month? When I got to Angelo's table, I got my chance. I told a table full of *pisanos* that their ancestors had considered tomatoes poisonous. They looked me incredulously. Italians thought tomatoes were too bitter and acidic to eat. It wasn't until a Jewish doctor in early America convinced them that they were delicious when cooked, that the Italians in America started to think otherwise. He urged them to make this vine fruit a part of their ingredient options. Through his discovery, the word got back to Italy that tomatoes were perfect for sauces. From there, the cuisine of Italy took on another tasteful dimension. I reckoned that the Jews were entitled to a piece of the action. Compensation was in order. The way I figured, if the Jews had convinced the Italians to use tomatoes, which they do so delightfully, we should get a royalty settlement. My final offer to Bruno was that the Jews should be the official accountants for all Italian dishes that use red sauces, and that the Mob could do the promotion!

"Where do you come up with this information?" Bruno asked.

I laughed and said, "I read it on the inside paper wrapper of a Bubba Golden blintza package."

I informed Angelo, for his further edification, that when Israel produced its first ever-agricultural cash crop, Italy bought it all. Of course it was tomatoes!

"Now think about this deeply, because it is worth knowing. There might not be spaghetti sauce or pizza if a Jewish doctor in the early United States hadn't told his Italian friends what to do with this versatile amazing red fruit."

Angelo laughed at my story, slipped me a twenty spot, and said, "Pay me when you can."

When I got back to the table, everyone was wondering what I did to get the money. They couldn't wait to leave the restaurant. Of course, I had to leave the tip and decided to hang around. I thought that if

The Bunny Hop

Angelo was in a generous mood, I could ease the debt by getting out my best material. I rattled off a couple of my new jokes and Angelo said he'd book me at one of the clubs he had an "interest" in.

I jumped at the chance. I found myself opening up at a nearby comedy club. I varied my routine from night to night but always had some help. I loved hecklers, because they always made it easier.

I was up on stage one night, and I hadn't even said a word, but only been introduced, when a "fan" in the audience yelled out, "Hey what's going on behind the curtains?"

"Nothing at all," I said, trying to fend off his challenge.

"Come on," he said. "Something is really happening behind the curtains."

By now, he has the whole audience looking all over for signs of activity behind me.

"I absolutely assure you there is nothing going on behind the curtains." I was emphatic.

Then he struck, "Well, there certainly is nothing happening in front of the curtains."

It was a proven technique: Get buried, and then get redemption, and I was doing it nightly. Mr. Bruno loved my little skits and paid me handsomely. I was grateful or his support and felt I was moving swiftly in the right direction when I got an unexpected call. It was my father warning me about what I was getting into. Everyone in town knew exactly who Angelo was, even my father. His warning went unheeded. Angelo had been nothing but a gentleman to me. That was the last time I ever talked to my father. Ironically, after that, Angelo became my surrogate father. He gave me great advice on how to treat women, and how to make what he called a "presentation." He felt women were God's greatest gift, and we should be aware of that by giving them gifts constantly. We should always remind them how beautiful they are to our eyes and how important they are to our hearts.

I was proud to take the money I earned from him and put it in the pot at home, as long as I could have enough to make my dates with Judi special. I was sticking to my guns and keeping my dream alive. I made a secret bond with Angelo. He promised he would always look after me, and he expected my trust and confidence in return. I accepted, and my bounty was a beautiful gold watch that made a lot of people nervous.

ANGELO "GENTILE DON" BRUNO

"MY MENTOR"

BOB HORN

In 1952, I felt like everything was peaking nicely. I was a teenage TV star, which was as close to being a teen idol as you could be in Philly in those days. I had reveled in the success of the Bunny Hop, which to this day is the most enduring dance in America, as it is performed at all sorts of social occasions. It gives me a lot of pride to look back at that now, but I knew exactly what I was doing then. I felt like I was in complete control. My relationship with Bob Horn was great. He agreed to write me a letter of recommendation that helped get me into Columbia University, even though I didn't have all the credits I needed to be accepted. I found that interesting, because Bob never went to college, but because of what he had achieved, an institution as esteemed as Columbia thought very highly of his words. He was the first ever disc jockey to be honored by the world famous Jewish organization, B'nai Brith, and I was the one who got to award him this honor when I was President of Ellis Gimbel AZA fraternity in 1953. Oddly, when I first applied to get into the fraternity, I was turned down even though they had rules to accept Jews. Within a year, I was the frat's president.

I had the girl of my dreams on my arm. Mr. Bruno was going to be my back-up whenever I needed his guidance. I was getting offers to produce radio shows. I was starting to make money on my own and could continue to live in fine style. It looked like everything was going to get even better. I went shopping for an engagement ring and eyeballed one that even Angelo was impressed by. I wanted to propose

The Bunny Hop

to Judi before I went away to college to make sure she was still my girl, even if I had to leave Philly and go to New York. It was only ninety minutes away. If I needed to get back to Philly, I could be back in a flash

I had a feeling that New York was going to be in my plans a lot more, especially since there was talk that NBC was interested in buying into Bandstand and bringing the show to New York. They wanted to put the famed TV program into the living rooms of the whole nation. This delighted the executives at WFIL, who could smell the money coming. NBC wined and dined Bob Horn and brought him to New York to see their network studios. Mr. Horn went and didn't like what he saw. Instead of jumping at the chance to become a national celebrity, he thought the studio was too small and there wouldn't be enough room to accommodate all the kids he loved to have on the show. To the surprise of his bosses in Philadelphia, he refused to be part of taking the show to New York, and it killed the deal.

It's never been wise to insult the ones who sign your paycheck, but what Bob Horn did to the executives was to spit in their faces. He was still a big enough celebrity to pull this power play off, but I knew he was playing with fire. I also knew there was no love lost between Bob Horn and the executives at WFIL. They were no fans of Bob's, but he made them a ton of money. They were jealous he had such power over their investment, and I thought it was just a matter of time before the "suits" would try to get rid of him.

"Payola" was becoming part of the vernacular, and most disc jockeys at the big radio stations had already learned to deal with the promo-men and the perks. When Bob Horn turned up with a brand new Cadillac, there was a lot of speculation as to which record company had paid for it. Bob Horn was starting to believe his own hype, and honestly, he deserved it, too. He was that good

Bob Horn was such a tremendous innovator and a huge success at everything he did. He had an incredible work ethic and always had several projects going at the same time. He was hired by Jack Steck at WFIL in 1949, originally to be a daytime announcer readings news, weather reports, and public service announcements. He also landed a night-time music show where he indulged in his "hobby." He played mostly big band and jazz records and displayed a skillful, yet relaxed, style on the air. As his popularity grew, he was given better time slots. In just a couple of years, he had turned his hobby into the most important music show in the hottest music town. He was a star, and I came to idolize the man, as I mentioned before. When television entered America's living rooms, Bob Horn, a radio guy through and through, made the transition a rocket ride in Philly. Many thought he had a face for radio, but he was an average looking man, except for his height. He stood six feet tall, which was large in those days. He always wore suits and, to most, looked more like a businessman than an entertainment celebrity. He was a family man with children, and his vices were cigarettes and alcohol, which he discreetly hid in the beginning.

When the television version of Bandstand first aired 1952, the show was admittedly dull and lackluster. His program was filled with "sound clips," which were the equivalent of today's videos. Bob Horn was the first to take advantage of these performances. Usually taken from movies where an artist or a band would perform a song, or made specifically for theater audiences, these visuals were lifted and broadcast on TV shows as if they were singles. They helped promote the movie, the artist, and the whole music business in general, which was dominated by the big publishers. Back in those days, the publishers had the power the major record companies have now. They paid the songwriters for their creations, matched the songs with the artist, paid the artist modest fees, and kept the rest for themselves. It wasn't until copyright laws were restructured years later that they lost their stranglehold on the music business. What Bob was doing was benefiting the publishers greatly, and they knew it. These "clips" were fun to watch, but they couldn't carry a full show.

When Bob Horn became the first broadcaster to put dancing teenagers on television, he was merely doing it to give the audience a chance to be a part of the show and make the program more intimate. I don't think he realized that nearly fifty years later it would be so entrenched in Americana, with shows like American Bandstand and Soul Train, by making the dancing segments the most visual parts of their presentations. What Bob Horn did was liven up his show and let the kids in Philly have some fun. He also created the "rate a record" segment where actual audience members would listen to a new song and give their opinions. But what made Bob so special was the way he handled the artists. He always made them feel so welcomed, and when he spotted a fresh new talent, he would be very supportive, often giving these rising stars their initial lift-offs. Everything Bob did promoted music in front of a hungry audience. When he had artists come down to sing their songs in front of the Bandstand crowd, he was opening up another form of promotion the record companies and publishers had not yet fully exploited. He expanded his efforts beyond television to promoting live concert shows. Through his power and vision, he could put a new artist on the radio, television, or even in a ballroom for a live concert, all in one swoop. Plus, his promotion did wonders for the new television retail business, when TVs were considered non-essential and only for the rich. He helped bust up that perception. Nobody anywhere had this much power and prestige, or the ability to break an artist.

Whether they wanted to or not, and most often they wanted to, the record companies and publishers would line up to get Bob Horn's blessing on their records and artists. He showed great musical integrity and picked his favorites wisely. Sadly, he had to pass on a lot of acts he felt were unoriginal or not ready for a mass audience. From 1952 to 1956, Bob Horn was one of the most powerful people in the music industry, even though he was not one of their employees. In those days the nation's radio stations played "follow the leader." A lot of stations would play a song specifically because Bob Horn was playing it on Bandstand. In a way, he was a one-man radio tip sheet! It put Bob in a daring and precarious position. If he would not give into the temptation of payola and all the perks offered to him, he could have kept his power base in tact for years. Instead Bob Horn, by his own admission, "pushed the envelope" too much.

He started carousing around and was now drinking heavily. He felt invisible. He even noticed how the executives were scheming to get rid of him, and he ignored their plots. They repeatedly forced him to take on co-hosts, but that never worked. They complained about his "plain" look, saying he didn't have the style of a TV star. They continued to rant on and on about how he spoiled their network shot. Through it all, Bob Horn just kept getting busier and busier. He created an adult version of Bandstand that very much resembled late night television today, where the artists would tell their jokes, sing their songs, and sit down next to the host and chat. Bob Horn was working himself to death and burning the candle at both ends. Everybody could see what was coming, even Bob Horn, but he wouldn't acknowledge it.

He was busted for "driving tipsy" and prosecuted even when there really weren't laws to that effect at the time. It was clear that he was being set up for a fall, but he was so popular that he'd have to commit a very heinous crime in order for popular opinion to sway against him. In the end, Bob Horn did his bosses a huge favor when he got caught with a fifteen-year old girl. It was an ugly and complicated trial, and he was finally sentenced to six months in federal prison. When he got out of jail, nobody in the entertainment business wanted to have anything to do with him. He was ostracized, and rightly so, many thought. He hit rock bottom when one night after dinner, he went into the bathroom and put a gun in his mouth.

His wife Ann walked in and said, "So, you're going to leave me and the girls here alone. Well then go ahead and do it!"

He pulled the gun out of his mouth, put it back in the drawer, and decided to move his family across the country to get a fresh start. Eventually, he ended up in Houston, Texas, where he went back to sales. He tried being a disc jockey under an assumed name but couldn't make that work. So, he returned to sales and once again became a great success. He became able to afford his family the luxury of raising show horses. He was a complete family man in his later years and quite happy, at that, although he still had contempt and bitterness for those in the music world who froze him out. He admitted he had done wrong, but always thought his talent would save him. It didn't.

He died of a massive heart attack after dinner one night in 1966; he was just over fifty years old. It had been said that his funeral was paid for by one of the early dancers on the Bandstand show. That rumor is unequivocally not true. Bob Horn's family paid for his funeral, and anyone making statements to the contrary is being disingenuous.

Does Bob Horn belong in the Rock and Roll Hall Of Fame? Absolutely. Will he be enshrined? Probably not. For all of his considerable contributions to our popular musical culture, it's easy for one to say they don't want any pedophiles to be honored. It's sad to all of those who can appreciate Bob Horn's worth. Alan Freed imitated him, and many others of lesser talents have become millionaires off of what Bob Horn created. Yet, most music fans today don't even know who he is. In Philadelphia, he'll never be forgotten. The City of Brotherly Love thinks the Rock and Roll Hall of Fame doesn't belong in Cleveland. Instead, it should have been built in Philadelphia, the first place where it would have had a much greater chance of being commercially successful. If the Hall of Fame was in Philly, Bob would have a shot.

BREAKING OUT

    I was finishing high school during the early Bandstand years, and I had to make up class credits in order to enter Columbia University in the fall of 1953. The summers were usually easy for me. They were a time when I could indulge even more in my avocations, hoping to truly turn them into my vocation. This summer, I had to bust my *touche* to get up to speed. However, I would never miss my Saturday night dates with Judi. We had been together for two full years now, and I was determined to keep the bond strong, even while I was going away to chase my dreams. I was working harder than I ever had, trying to make up for all the classes I missed. What kept me going was my "reward," seeing Judi. We kept up the pace; going to nice restaurants, catching some great shows, and no matter what, always having a ton of fun.
    In the two years that I had spent with Judi, I had come to admire her so much. She was one of the smartest girls in the whole school system, and she had her heart set on becoming a lawyer. I had no doubt she was going to make it, despite the fact that women were discouraged to try and enter the legal system, then. I felt in so many ways we were finding out a lot about each other and she was helping me grow. She had incredible diction and spoke with perfect grammar and confidence. Often, she would correct something I said, but I honestly didn't mind. If I was going to have a career in radio or television, I wanted to be as prepared as possible. I knew a command of the language was vital in order for me to achieve my goals. When I said "wahta" instead of "water," Judi would stop me in the middle of sentences until I knew

the correct pronunciation. She was so good, that if I was butchering Yiddish, which is nearly impossible to do because the language is so coarse, she'd still correct me. It forced me to speak concisely and clearly, something I in which I still take pride. Judi was a great listener, and she had to be, because everybody who knows me knows I never shut up. She was so very supportive of my dreams and goals, while the members of my family always had some doubt. They would be happy if my fortunes were up, but the second I hit a dry spell, I'd get the *schpeal:* "Go get a day job."

Judi hung in there the entire time, and that meant a lot to me. I confessed everything to her. I wanted to be a disc jockey, an actor, a big band leader, and even a songwriter. And although I put on quite a show, I really was an introvert at heart, one dying for attention. I loved being on-stage, but I wasn't too fond of crowds and parties. I liked smaller, more intimate gatherings.

Judi had so much class. She was always well dressed. Even if we were wearing sports clothes, she'd still look better than everyone else. She took great care of the finest little details. She was always well made-up, and her hair and perfume were very tasteful. I loved to tell her that at five foot three inches tall, with dark brown eyes and a "coke bottle" figure, she was setting off a biological bomb inside me.

We could talk about anything, and our relationship was very open. She was very well read and worldly, even as a teenager. She spoke with warmth, class, and sophistication, and anyone could tell she was raised very well. I could sense this confidence in her whenever we were together. As much as I cared for her, I think I respected her even more.

I knew that it was going to be a tough road leaving Philly during the week, but good things are always hard to achieve. When we first met at the Bar Mitzvah for her aunt's son, I was sixteen, and she was only fourteen. I thought she was more mature than I at the time, but I felt like I caught up a lot in two years, and that evened the playing field between us. I was always tall for my age, and people often thought I was older than I was. Judi got the same treatment, because she was so intelligent. But, she was already a woman when I first met her, and she became even more incredible during the high school years.

Her mother was my antagonist, but she was always very polite. I was always on my best behavior when I came by to pick up Judi. I asked once again if we could see each other on Friday nights, but I was denied. Thankfully, Judi was willing to go to the Beth Shalom on Sunday afternoons, where we met, so we could spend just a bit more time together. We'd dance, joke, and have a good time, sometimes even when we were all worn out from a really great time the night before. Later, we found a secret hideaway. Only seeing Judi on Saturdays and Sundays was not enough. After getting out of Olney High School each day, Judi would attend a Hebrew High School that was down near Temple University. She'd take the Broad Street subway downtown, and after her classes, we'd meet at a little soda shop across from her Hebrew school. Sometimes, we only had fifteen minutes for each other, and often I sacrificed an opportunity just to see her. We both felt limited by her mother's restrictions but knew we'd have hell to pay if her mother ever caught us. Then, at night when I would faithfully call her, we hardly ever spoke for less than an hour. Fridays were absolute torture. I never asked if she dated anyone else. I didn't want to know. I wondered if she was out with her friends, but not being with her was really tough. If I had my druthers, I would have just taken Friday off of everybody's calendars. I knew in my heart that there would be one day when Judi could speak for herself, and that would be my nirvana. Until then, I had to play by the rules. I found this odd because in every other aspect of my life, I had been impatient and had pushed the package, but this time, I was willing to go very slowly in order to come home a winner. I was the turtle racing the hare.

One night, as I was getting ready for our date, I made reservations at a fancy restaurant and asked for the best table in the place. I had a clean, fresh, newly acquired haircut. I showered, shaved, and picked out my best Mohair sweater, a pair of crisply pressed slacks, and brightly shined shoes. I wasn't dressed to kill, I was dressed to be loved! When I tied the perfect knot in my tie, I felt so good! I did this every time I went out with Judi. I wanted to look special. I usually called over to Judi before I drove over, but on this night I was running a little late, so I waited. The phone rang, and I waited for my mother to pick it up. She didn't, so I had to run down the hall to get it. The phone might ring fifteen times sometimes, but if someone was home, we'd answer it. When I got there, I picked it up and I said hello. It was Judi, so I was pleased.

As soon as I heard her start to speak though, I knew something was not kosher. She did not sound like she usually did. She was not cheerful, and that felt odd. She was being so tentative and quiet. I stayed as calm as I could and was giving her my undivided attention, hoping that she was just upset about something that would blow over. Then, she blew me away.

"Harvey," she said really quietly into the phone, "I can never see you again!"

I couldn't talk. I didn't even know how to start talking, so I just listened. I had never even entertained the thought that Judi would give up on me. It just didn't add up. She was polite and articulate, but I was melting from the inside out. The longer I listened, the more I felt the words weren't hers, and I started to feel bitterness along with the sadness. It was obvious she wasn't interested in my rebuttal; she did all of the talking. As I listened to her, I kept asking myself, "Why is she being taken from me? I have done nothing to deserve this."

She started to loosen up a bit after we'd been talking for about half an hour. We spoke softly to each other and reminded ourselves of all the great memories we had shared from those two years. I remember the feeling I had when my grandfather died. I had realized that I would never see him again, and now I remembered how much that hurt. I didn't want to hang up. If I was going to lose Judi, I was going to die talking to her on the telephone. I could feel my voice tremble with pain, and I struggled with the anger and angst I also felt, but still I wanted to speak softly and keep her on the phone. I couldn't keep her though. She said, "Goodbye," and she hung up on me. It was not in anger, but it was something she had never done to me before.

I let the telephone slowly slip out of my hands, and it took a couple of tries before I could get it back in its cradle. I crumbled to my knees and cried as much as I ever had in my life. I slowly got undressed and put on a pair of khakis, something I would never be seen wearing in public, and went out for a drive. The whole time I kept thinking about what Judi and I would have been doing and how I would try to steal a kiss every time I could. I never felt so empty, so alone. The longer I was sad, the angrier I got. I felt deep down inside that it was Judi's mother who forced her, against her will, to say goodbye to me. I just knew it, and nobody could convince me otherwise, but I really didn't have proof.

When I got home from my drive my mother said, "My, you're home early. Did you two have a fight?"

Judi and I never fought, so why would she think that?

"What? " I asked.

"I never did like her stuck up, pushy mother."

Again I asked, "What?"

"I gave her a piece of my mind the other day when she made some snide remarks about you, Harvey. I called her up, and she was going on and on about how you were spoiling Judi with all of your favors and the dates. She acted so ungrateful; it disgusted me!"

I spoke up. "You talked with Judi's mother the other day?"

"Talked to her? I chewed her ass out for being so shallow and behind the times."

"In other words, you made her so mad she took Judi away from me! How could you do such a thing?" Now, I was completely furious at my mother, too. I had nothing left. Judi was gone, my mother was the probable cause, and I felt I was going away to school for nothing. It was the "be all and end all" for me. I felt like I could trust no one.

When I calmed down, I decided to attack the problem. I wasn't going to just fade away. I would be seen. I would be out in public, so I would have to see Judi and look her in the eyes, so I could find out if this really was her decision. I knew that if I could look into her beautiful eyes again, they wouldn't lie to me. I tried to telephone her at odd hours at home, hoping she would answer the phone, but she never answered, and I had to hang up. I was very close to her cousin, Marty, so I sent word over through him, but I got no response. I kept going to the B'Nai Brith Shalom, but Judi never returned. I felt so forlorn.

Finally, I found an ally. The Bar Mitzvah where I met Judi was for her aunt's son. I saw her aunt, and when she learned what had happened, she was really angry and couldn't believe her sister was capable of such an indiscretion. I pleaded my case to Judi's aunt. She encouraged me to fight harder, which I did. I got a lot of sympathy, but I got no results. I just couldn't believe I would not see Judi in public, because there were only so many places you could go. I thought she probably couldn't go out at all anymore, because I never saw her.

I turned off the spotlight. I stopped searching for Judi on every street. I even entertained the thought that she'd moved away or gone off to college. I knew I would never, ever see her again. I was walking out of the Academy Of Music downtown one night, and my mind still full of the beautiful music I had just heard. Like most concert-goers, I wasn't paying much attention as I walked out into the night and wound down from a great show. I bumped into someone on the sidewalk and felt jostled out of my stride. I was taken aback. It was Judi! She turned around and kept walking faster and faster. I came up beside her and tried to get her attention. I waved in her face, but she turned her head and looked down.

"It's me, Judi!" I could not get her attention in any way. I walked for blocks beside her, I was so desperate. I only wanted to look in her eyes and see that they meant good-bye, but I was being denied that courtesy! She wouldn't speak to me, and she practically ran away from me. To this day, I don't know what I did to hurt her. It was emotional torture seeing her. It was as if the same wound from the night she called to say good-bye had been ripped back open, but this time it was with a bigger knife! That was the last time I ever saw her.

THE HARVEY SHELDON BIG BAND

I made a lot of connections during the Bandstand years and tried to parlay that into a full-time career. I took a job producing Eddie Newman's radio show. Then, I was asked to go back to TV. At one time, the management had paired Lee Stewart with Bob Horn on Bandstand, but that hadn't worked out. A rival TV station across town, WDEL, wanted to compete with Bandstand. So, they brought Lee over to do a knock-off show. When Lee offered me the job as his producer, I first checked with Bob Horn, and he gave me his blessing, even if I was going to be competition for him. Lee's show was a moderate success, and I was learning a lot about the business, but I was always looking around for bigger and better opportunities. I really wanted a network gig where I could go "national," as we said in those days. I got a huge break when Jimmie Komack recommended me for a part Red Button's network TV show on NBC, and I got it without an audition.

I was cast on Red's show for the 1953-54 season and found out that not only was a network show a lot more fun and a lot more work, but it paid a lot better, too. For the first time, I was making really good money. Television was inventing itself in those days, and nobody really knew how big and powerful a medium it would become. I knew I wanted to stay on the air as much as possible. At the end of 1954, my role was over and I went back to radio, which was always a home for me. I did know that both radio and television were a roller coaster ride with many stops and starts on a never ending track. I was prepared to go wherever necessary in order to get my real shot.

JOINT IS JUMPIN

THE HARVEY SHELDON BIG BAND

I ended up back in Philly and took a job as a disc jockey on WHAT, with a Jazz show at night. WHAT was a Black radio station, but I fit right in. The show became a hang-out for musicians. The clubs usually closed at midnight, and my show ran from midnight until 5:00AM. I had an open-door policy and invited musicians to come down to the station after their shows to hang out, play records, and talk. One of the regulars was a young saxophone player who had been in Sticks McGee's band. He would confess to me that he wanted to put all of his energy into jazz and make his mark as a serious musician. Often, he would give me tips on how bands worked and song structure, along with other helpful advice about music in general. I had no idea that he would become such an icon, but John Coltrane was always willing to chat with anyone interested in music. Many a night he'd stay for the whole show, and we'd drive down to Horn and Hardart's for breakfast to keep the conversation going.

The more I learned about music, without really being a musician, the more I wanted to get involved. My stage experience had only included acting, stand-up comedy, and dancing. I started to get visions in my head of my own big band. Rock and roll had hit America in the mid-fifties and pulverized everything in its path. I hated to see Big Band music getting trampled like it did, and I wanted to keep fighting in my own way to keep it alive. I was making my living playing jazz records, but even as popular as jazz was, it had taken a backseat to rock and roll. I'll admit I was a bit jealous of rock and roll in the beginning, and I was surprised it came out of the pack to be the champion. I saw Philadelphia as the crossroads for the musical world in the early fifties. Jazz, Swing, Big Bands, and Pop music were all fighting for the limelight, while Rock and Roll came out of nowhere and blew the competition away. The only solace I could take out of this development, was that Bill Haley was from Chester, Pennsylvania, just outside of Philly, and was a regular in the club scene.

I had no idea how to put a big band together. Most of the people I knew said, "Just put the word out." So I did. Philly was a town where everybody knew everybody. Although it was America's third most populated city in those days, it still had a small-town feel to it, and also had another nickname, besides "The City Of Brotherly Love." Philly was also called "The City of Homes" because of the rows and

The Bunny Hop

rows of houses surrounding downtown. There were a lot of distinct neighborhoods, but it was really easy to get around town, and most of the entertainment was downtown. Just walking the streets at night, you would surely see a cache of great musicians.

My vision was an eighteen-piece band, minimum. I wanted the groove to be a cross between Benny Goodman's famous band and Woody Herman's Third Herd, but even more hip. I wanted to integrate more jazz musicians and give it a real new feel. I was hearing a fresh new sound in my head, and I wanted to go about getting it. I had a limited knowledge of musical arrangement, but a lot of guts and *chutzpeh*. There were so many great musicians in town, but most of them had day gigs and families, along with society gigs on the weekends, so I had to get really creative in order to attract them to my dream band.

I was asking for a lot. I could offer no salary, and I had a limited ability to write and score music, but I had a sound that was exploding inside my brain and wouldn't let me rest. How could an unknown, with no résumé, attract the musicians needed to flesh out this musical skeleton? All I had was a pile of charts with adaptations of songs I wanted to do, as well as some new ideas. I had no sheet music that any well-known musician would recognize. It would be gibberish to them, but to me, it was a gold mine. I had put the word out that I was going to get a big band together, and surprising enough, it was taken seriously.

My friends in the musical community started to inquire where I was going with this new musical adventure. I knew I had to do something that was significantly different than what was being created around town in order to employ the best players without pay!

All I was asking for was great players to work and rehearse for free, who would then play my music and get paid at the gig. I had to be very creative with my pitches each time I found a musician I wanted. As much as I was begging, I actually may have been underestimating my influence and connections. My jazz show had legs, and musicians knew I was "down." I was savvy as to who the hot players, songwriters, and developing new talent were. Then, I connected with Billy Root.

I was so lucky. He looked at my wad of papers and didn't laugh at me; that was a first! He took me seriously! He told me I was "almost there" and that he would re-write my arrangements without compromising my vision. I felt like God was blessing my band. Billy Root was perfect. He had the temperament to handle anyone and was a musical genius. He could tell by looking at my rough sketches that I had a really good painting in the works, so he jumped on board. He would be the arranger from the tenor sax position, and I hired myself to be the conductor, comedian, accountant, recruiter, and public relations director. I asked around and found out what the going wage was for big band musicians. I then promised anyone who joined my band that they would be paid accordingly. Then, the bonfire began.

Billy's respected reputation, having played with Woody Herman and Stan Kenton, opened a lot of doors. I have always been a dreamer, but I hate to see society's old habits hold my hopes back. I found out there were two musicians' unions in Philadelphia. One had White musicians, one had Black musicians, and they both had different rules. I did everything I could to entice Black jazz musicians into my band, but the powers-that-be were not ready for a merger. I was denied. Here I was in the most progressive musical city in the world, and I couldn't hire some really good friends with whom I wanted to work. It hurt.

My band started to flesh out. I landed Frank Young on drums, and he was spectacular. His resumé included a stint with Stan Kenton. Soon, I had Joe Goldberg on trombone and John Bono on sax, both of whom had played with Woody Herman and Benny Goodman. Later, we added Vinnie Tanno on trumpet. I trusted Billy Root implicitly; I knew that from a musical and personal standpoint, he could spot the right guys. We found a rehearsal stage in downtown Philly near Broad and South streets, and we practiced at every chance we could. We started to draw a crowd to our rehearsals, and word spread that a great new band was on the horizon. When the band was good and ready, I had to find places we could play, and times that fit everybody's schedule. We looked to the colleges where our music was still popular. Philadelphia has more universities than any other major city, and we played them all: Penn State, Temple, LaSalle, Villanova, etc.

I took advantage of my Jewish roots and booked the band at many *shulfights*. These were Sunday afternoon gatherings sponsored by the Synagogues. We had to play at least three traditional Jewish numbers to which the crowd could dance the *fralich*. Billy quickly arranged the songs in our style for the band, and we got a great reaction at these gigs.

I usually had to placate the local Rabbi who often came over to me and asked if we could be a little *bissal* (softer). I told him that we weren't a society band, we were a jazz band, and I left it at that. I followed Benny Goodman's advice to "never compromise."

Another time, I was asked if we knew any "novelty songs." I answered that query by telling the entertainment director that my band didn't play any stupid songs! If they wanted Spike Jones, then they should book Spike Jones. I got really close with Billy, Joe, John and Vinnie, and they respected me for not compromising their integrity. We played colleges on Friday and Saturday nights and the *shulfights* on Sunday nights. It made for a busy weekend, but we were making some great music. I also wanted to add a personal touch to each show.

I would do some of my comedy *shtick* before the band would play, to warm up the audience. This was particularly effective before the Jewish audiences, who may not have been prepared for the rocking band we had. One club owner was so enthralled with our band, that he gave us a steady booking and insisted we name his club "The Harvey Sheldon All-Star Big Band" for the night. We were getting rave reviews. One reporter for the Philadelphia Bulletin wrote, "The last time I experienced such a musical happening was when Benny Goodman used to play the Earl Theater."

We were hot! We had one show in Philly where we peaked. All of the musicians were in their prime, and I could hardly believe the musical heights they took me to that night. The crowd was jitterbugging and tearing the place up. I couldn't have been any happier, but still, it led me to think. Judi had to have heard about these shows. I wondered if she ever would come. I spent many nights looking for her, and I looked especially hard at the *shulfights,* thinking I had a better chance to see her there.

We were definitely a good enough band to make records and be signed to a major label, but when we went looking for a deal, the record companies were dumping big bands left and right. The financial people at the record labels noticed how much more money they could make off rock and roll acts that were a lot smaller and less expensive, than working with a big band. It started getting harder to find gigs, and it became a losing proposition. I hated to see it all go away, but I saw how Las Vegas was offering musicians more money than I could offer, and I knew it was a matter of time before my band would be pillaged. Forty years later, I caught up with Frank Leone, who had seen my big band a number of times and eventually arranged songs for Paul Anka and Englebert Humperdink.

Currently, he is the President of the Musicians Union of Las Vegas. He was a young musician on the scene and wanted to see all the bands in town. He told me that he fondly remembered the thrilling sounds of my jazz band, but his last thought really got to me. Frank said, "Had the forces of the changing pop music scene not been so powerfully overwhelming, then surely Harvey's band would have come into its own as a jazz entity." I am still extremely flattered by Frank's kind remarks, but I honestly think he was right.

We booked a show at one of our favorite clubs, and I was giving the band a quick break. I used to sing a couple of numbers, and although the majority of our shows were filled instrumental numbers and standards, we had worked up our own style. I was looking all over the crowd for Judi. I had a funny feeling about this show, and I thought she might be there. When I started to sing my songs, my voice cracked all over the place, and I completely lost my control of my pitch. When the song was over, I was so embarrassed that I made a joke trying to stave off all the boos. I quickly shouted out, "Spike Jones, I'm available!" That got me a laugh and covered my ass. We finished the show by doing a spirited version of the "Bunny Hop," which had the whole room swinging in one big conga line. We went off the stage with a great big bang.

It was the last show we would ever do, and I gave up looking for Judi.

Harvey Sheldon hosting his sports TV show.

LOVE SONGS

By 1960, I had moved on to WEEZ in Philadelphia and was drawing some impressive ratings. Radio was now being audited for listeners by sponsors and getting a little more sophisticated and commercial. Billboard magazine was firmly established as the pop music bible, listing the best selling records, as well as the song play lists of the major radio stations. I sent my play list in weekly, just as any other jock would do, and I took pride in my selections. I was visited by many of the great record promoters of the era, and I made some valuable connections that would help me for years to come.

I still had music in my blood, even if my ego was a bit wounded from the end of my big band, so I started to write songs for myself that I wasn't ready to show anybody. I thought it might be good for me if I gave dating another try and stopped letting the ashes be my reality. I had just had my appendix removed and was going to Dr. Bernstein's office to have the stitches taken out. I walked into the reception room, and in the far corner of the room was a lovely young lady. I was captured by her beauty. She was a dead ringer for Kim Novak. I tried to get a better look at her without getting caught.

Dr. Bernstein had been my doctor since I was nine years old, so I knew him pretty well. When it was my turn to go into his office, I said, "That mouse is a super gasser." My good doctor thought he had a rodent infestation. When I told him that "gasser" and "mouse" were terms of affection for pretty women, he started laughing. I had to ask him another question. Could he get me her phone number? I had to

The Bunny Hop

take her out. Sure enough, he scribbled her number on a prescription pad and handed it to me. When I got to the radio station, I called her right away and told her who I was. Her name was Marsha Lewin, and she laughed when she found out how I got her phone number. We didn't talk for very long on the phone, because I was calling her when I was on the air doing my radio show.

For me, it was love at first sight. I felt like I had to impress her, but I found out she was just sixteen. She looked a lot more mature than that. I was twenty-three at the time but didn't see any reason why I shouldn't see her and ask for dates. I thought she would say no, but she said yes, and we hit it off great from the start. We dated only on Saturday nights but never missed one date for a year and a half. I couldn't stop buying her gifts, and I was on top of the world. I knew that, in show business, it's hard to have a normal relationship with all of the long hours, ups and downs, and rejections, but I wanted to give it a try.

Marsha would inspire me to compose a full Broadway musical. I called it, "Marsha, I Love You." A lot of musicals featured women's names and were very successful. I was getting a lot of praise and support. My mafia friend Angelo Bruno was thrilled with my creation, and he arranged for financial backing to put the show into production. Bruno was totally convinced that I had a hit show. We planned to debut it in Philly with the hope that the musical would make the transition to Broadway.

Marsha and I continued our torrid love affair, and I treated her to a glamorous life in Philadelphia. We ate at the finest establishments and supper clubs. We saw a lot of great acts together including Tony Martin, Vic Damone, Sammy Davis Jr., the Four Aces, the Mills Brothers, Tony Bennett, the Four Lads, Jo Stafford, and Kay Starr, along with many Broadway shows and jazz concerts.

I asked Marsha to join me on a boat trip I planned to Miami Beach, where I was negotiating the rights to buy a radio and TV station. On the journey we could buy the appropriate yacht wear and have a grand time. There would be a lot of dining and dancing. I felt like I had finally met someone who could understand my fascination with show biz.

Marsha's birthday was July 4th, so we planned to fly back to Philadelphia for the special occasion. The entire trip was full of romance.

The weather was beautiful; every night seemed to be a full moon with a sky full of stars, along with music and great times. I was in love.

Our rendezvous in Philly was to be at a famous Italian restaurant we loved. All the stars were lined up. I got to know Marsha's family well. Even though her parents were divorced, I saw both of them quite often and felt comfortable around them. I knew they were not a family with a lot of means, but I was certain my success in show business would offer Marsha a great life. I made arrangements to pay for her college education at the University of Pennsylvania, something her family could not afford. I was dying to see the look in her eyes when I surprised her.

Bruno made the reservations at the restaurant. We finished our trip in fine style and headed back home for our celebration. Bruno was anxious to hear the last few songs I'd composed, and I missed my friend and mentor. I knew I'd written something that would establish me as a legit Broadway composer.

When we got to the fine Italian eatery, the wonderful aroma of Italian spices was in the air, and I couldn't wait to dig in. Bruno was sitting at the head of the table, and Marsha and I were set to be the guests of honor. This was going to be her best birthday ever and my finest hour.

When Marsha entered the room, she was ravishing. I was taken aback by her beauty. She was maturing into one of the most gorgeous women on Earth. The moment that I first saw her in the doctor's office popped into my mind. She was stunning then, and I couldn't believe she could find another way to take my breath away.

We all awaited her placement at the table. Marsha was introduced to all of the friends Bruno had invited to celebrate the day God gave her breath. When we sat down, Marsha leaned over to me and said she needed to speak with me. I couldn't wait to give her my birthday present and her scholarship. Instead, I got a knife through the heart.

"Harvey, you create beautiful music and lyrics, and I know they are about me. However, in real life you may not be able to create what you want."

Then she dropped the bomb.

"I never, ever want to see you again." She got up and walked away. I couldn't move. I couldn't give her my presents. My eyes teared up immediately, and I felt like my heart would stop.

As Marsha walked away, Bruno jumped up and raced after her. As I was fighting my emotions, Bruno was looking for a logical solution, mafia style. He stopped her. He made every attempt to convince her to come back to the table and speak with me, but she refused. After she left, Bruno came back to the table and told me what she said. I had trouble fighting back the tears.

"Harvey, I tried," Bruno said. "She wouldn't budge. She said that your music is all-consuming and that there is no room for her in your life."

I was shocked, because I had given Marsha all of my affection. I gave her everything. Then, Bruno delivered the hay-maker.

He leaned over and whispered in my ear, "She told me she loves you, and I should look after you because you are a helluva nice guy."

That did it. I had to cry.

I knew I would never, ever see her again.

Marsha inspired me to write great melodies and lyrics, but my heartache got in the way. The musical I thought was my masterpiece ended up never being performed. Angelo would not be my producer, and that hurt a lot. I felt I'd let everybody down.

I took awhile, but I recovered and I started writing again. I found a way to get back to the piano keys with a pen, but I didn't know for whom to play my songs.

One day, when I was getting ready for my show, I had a visitor come by who wanted to plug his records. He was just one of many promo men I would meet over the years, but he became a great friend. Leroy Lovett had a long list of credits, and I admired him from afar. Now, I was getting to meet him in Harry Chips's office. He had gone from being an arranger with Duke Ellington to a record producer, and a very good one at that. I loved his records and easily found room for them on my radio show. I also regularly reported them to Billboard. Our relationship grew, and one day I got up the nerve to tell Leroy I had written some songs. I didn't expect him to show any interest. After all, disc jockeys usually aren't songwriters. If they were, they'd be artists. To my joy, he said he would be willing to listen to my ideas and would be honest with me about my creations.

Leroy invited me to his house in Overbrook, and as he sat at the piano and played around with some of my melodies, I could tell he liked them and knew I had some degree of talent. After a couple of minutes, we had a deal. We would write together. I couldn't believe my good fortune. Leroy had written some great songs like, "After the Lights go Down," a hit for Al Hibler. He also wrote "Can't I?" which was a big song for Nat King Cole. I had studied famous lyricists and songwriters both musically and historically, and I was keen to have my songs placed in Broadway shows. With Leroy by my side, I thought I had a chance now. He introduced me to many other artists and musicians, and what he said about Philadelphia was true: "Everybody knows everybody else in Philly."

Leroy took me down to the Black side of town, and I got to work with the Furness Brothers, who performed under the name of The Keys. I watched the five brothers work out arrangements for new songs and often was asked for my thoughts. I felt accepted when they took my suggestions seriously. They even rearranged a couple of their songs to the way I had suggested.

One of the things I noticed about some of the great writers I admired is that they had died so young. George Gershwin died at thirty-eight, Larry Hart at forty-four, Cole Porter died young. As I started to write, I feared that fate because I was now having excruciating headaches and pain in my hands that the doctors couldn't diagnose. They said it was all in my head!

They thought I was torturing myself. I gave up the boat I had bought and docked on the Potomac River, where I did a lot of entertaining, meeting some fabulous people. I cashed that out so I could buy some time. I was going to pour all of my energy into my writing and hope for the best. I quit my DJ job and applied for a radio station licenses in Miami and Boston. I thought that if I ran out of money; I could still run a radio station with the money I'd earned and saved. I was certain I could write better songs than what I heard on the radio.

While I was working with Leroy, I told him about Marsha.

He made a joke of it all when he said, "You write much better when you get dumped!"

I had to admit he was right. I was getting better and better. With Leroy's connections our songs were getting into the right hands.

The publishers were starting to lose their almighty power, as the record companies made more and more money on rock and roll. In those days, the leaders of big bands would be made available to the publishers at 8:00AM, and through a long day, they would go by and show them their songs. They would give the artist the sheet music, play it through on the piano, and the artist would either say yes or no. Sometimes there would literally be hundreds of song pluggers in line trying to get their songs in front of the great talent. Leroy was a big player in that scene and often could get right to an artist directly.

The musicians and bandleaders of that day were so professional and talented. They often could record side A of an album by lunch and finish the record before dinnertime. Everybody read music and was very well educated. There were stories that were proven to be true. For instance, Frank Sinatra was so good, he could literally sing a song perfectly the first time he ever saw it. That was the world in which we were competing. I hoped to be up to the test.

Leroy and I wrote ten songs together that I remember. "The Creator" was recorded, and we really wanted to get our songs to Nat King Cole, but he became ill and died far too young. I was very proud of my work, but when the publishers came along and offered me good money for a couple of my compositions, I took it and lost all of my credits and copyrights. I regret that I sold the songs I didn't write with Leroy, but I thought they would be just the start of many more to come.

In study of the music business and every aspect of it, I found an extraordinary combination that I think now I can explain. 95% of the musicians in my day were Black, Jewish, or Italian and there was a reason why. To the Italians, nothing is more glamorous than singing. An opera star is the highest form of star there is in Italy. I think that's why Italians are great singers. They aspire to it. The Jews, who do not allow instruments of any kind in a Synagogue, have always had to make do with just voice and lyrics. The Blacks have carried their folk culture wherever they have traveled through song. They did so without instruments, also. I think it is these inherent characteristics that made it so easy for the Black, Jewish, and Italian cultures to merge in the early twentieth century when America was stuck listening to aged music from Europe. These new immigrant groups wanted to keep their own cultures alive, but they also wanted to grow. I love Leroy's take on the subject: "If the Jews hadn't fallen in love with our music and not decided to get involved and help us write lyrics, you all would still be doing the minuet!"

There are a couple of reasons the partnership between the Jews and Blacks worked so wonderfully. The Jews were big admirers of blues and jazz as Leroy noted, but the inherent structures of their own ethnic songs were similar and recognizable to each other. The blues is based on one line, which is repeated twice and then followed by an answer. ("My baby left me, my baby left me, my baby she's gone.")

Then, it is repeated and answered differently. ("My baby left me, my baby left me, she said she's done.") It's a pattern, based on twelve bars, that just feels good. It's simple, compact, and conclusive, plus you can always whistle the melody.

The Jewish song structure is based on sixteen bar cycles. The Italians, however, use a single thread style in opera where very little, if anything, is repeated. So, when Jews first heard blues, it felt good to them; it made sense logistically. Likewise, when Blacks heard Jewish cantors, they felt comfortable with the structure. Together, the writers of the early part of the century put together the eight-bar format that became the standard form of western songwriting in the twentieth century. It's also the reason I didn't get more songs published or recorded. By 1960, that eight-bar style seemed outdated in the eyes of the record companies, and when the Beatles and Rolling Stones came along, it was almost like it was forgotten forever. I wasn't going to make anymore money writing songs, so I started thinking about new career options, when one day, my questions were answered for me. I got an FCC radio license to broadcast in Boston. I would have to leave Philly, but it was for the best.

I still love the songs that Leroy and I wrote, and I actually think with the advent of the Internet, somebody will see them, enjoy them, and probably record them. Thanks to Leroy, who found the sheet music, and with his blessing, I am publishing the lyrics to our songs in my autobiography. I hope you read them and enjoy them. Someday, I hope you will hear them as well.

I hoped Marsha would hear them, too.

The Bunny Hop

SINCE THE DAY I FOUND YOU

This is what I've always hoped for
This is a dream come true
Yes I'm drifting on a cloud-bank
Since the day I found you

Things have no rhyme or reason
Hold a special bliss
Doors that lead to happy places
Open when I feel your kiss

Smiles replace lonely teardrops
Faith is higher than a kite
And I know your love's unending
And everything will end just right

This is what I've always hoped for
This is a dream come true
Yes I'm drifting in heaven
Since the day I found you

Since the day I found you

Lyrics-Harvey Sheldon
Music-Leroy Lovett

Copyright 1958

LOVE SONGS

WHO

Who's gonna kiss you when it's lovin' time
Who's going to hug you when it's huggin' time
Who's going to hold your hand when it's holdin' time
Who? I tell you who
It's gonna be me

Who's going to make you warm when it's cold
Who's going to make you cool when it's hot
Who's never going to let you out of sight
Who? I tell you who
It's gonna be me

Wanna kiss your way through teardrops
 Brighten each teardrop with a smile
I'll never, never, never stop lovin' you
Who knows it's true better than you

I'm gonna be with you all the time
And try to make you happy all the time
Who's gonna love you till the end of time
Who? I tell you who
It's gotta be me

Lyrics: Harvey Sheldon
Music: Leroy Lovett

Copyright 1958 a ShelRoy song

The Bunny Hop

IN A DREAM

In a dream
Time is still
And you are by my side
We share love together
Like people in love would do
It's a paradise
That's what it is
And I'm lost in your kisses
Then I wake from dreaming
And my face wears a smile
It's because in a dream
You are mine for awhile

Lyrics: Harvey Sheldon
Music: Jet Winters/Leroy Lovett

Copyright Glen-Mark Pub

IT COULD BE HEAVEN

It could be heaven
If only you would love me
It could be heaven
If you would give your love to me
Won't you say the words
To make my every dream come true
Only little words
That say I love only you
If you let me share this night with you
Underneath the stars shining in the sky
We'll share the wonders and the joys of love
And drift till the moon rolls by
So if this is a dream
Don't wake me or my dream will end
This must be heaven
For this love I feel inside for you
And it's heaven here with you
And it's heaven here with you

Lyrics: Harvey Sheldon
Music: Leroy Lovett

Copyright 1961

The Bunny Hop

ONLY ONCE

Only once will the right one appear
The one that is meant for you
You…she'll be your own to have alone
This chance will come only once
Only once you will feel in your heart

The magic of boy meeting girl
She'll be your queen
The dream of a teen
You'll only know who she is
Only once

Her kiss will excite you
Your love will take off like a rocket
The touch of her hand will set you a glow
You'll feel like a million
With only a cent in you pocket
You'll never explain it
The miracle of it
But you will know only once
Only once, only once, only once, only once

Lyrics and Music
Sheldon/Burns

Copyright Glen Mark Publishing

MY LIFE, MY MEMORY

You ask me how much you mean to me
Really mean to me
And I can say that you're my life
My memory

You are my every single day
My tomorrows too
The only one
My life my memory

When you make love to me
You fill my soul with desire
With all my heart and soul
I know that your love will last

When your lips are close to mine
What can I do then
For you are my life
And my memories of you won't end

Lyrics: Harvey Sheldon
Music: Leroy Lovett

Copyright ShelRoy songs

The Bunny Hop

DREAMS AND ASHES

When I am smoking cigarettes
Te ashes in my tray
Are the remnants of the dreams
I have out away

Desires, we dreamed to get together
Only once spring was new
The only thing that mattered
Was my love for you

We fashioned all the future too
A pattern of our own
Where neither you or no I
Would know the meaning of love

When I kissed you lips we promised
In the dawn
Love would last forever and then
You were gone

So now I stir the ashes
There's room for doubt
My dreams are like cigarettes
And have to be put out

Lyrics: Harvey Sheldon
Music: Leroy Lovett

Copyright 1958

LOVE SONGS

APRIL IN MY HEART

Why do I look for flowers
And listen for the rain
As though my heart was waiting
For some magical refrain
You touched me
An our lips met
No word need they im-part
That's when you put April in my heart

I know it's September
Te calendar's not wrong
The autumn winds are blowing
An the days are growing long
I'm on my way to paradise
And your love gave me a start
When you put April in my heart

Lyrics: Harvey Sheldon
Music: Leroy Lovett

MarkMusic Inc. copyright 1958

PROMISE ME

Promise me your love and I will promise you my heart
I won't be afraid or ever be alone
Promise me your hand will always cling to mine
And in your arms tonight yes, I will be all right

Every day I'll be sharing your daily thoughts
And in each embrace, the tears, the laughter
Will shine in your face
Let me promise you my love every minute near or far
I'll belong to you and all other nights there are

Lyrics: Harvey Sheldon
Music: Leroy Lovett

LOVE SONGS

YOU LOVE HIM

You love him!
I know you love him
I hope he loves you
AS much as I love you

You need him
You say you need him
I hope he needs you
The way I need you

When he whispers in your ear
Do his words make you tingle
And when you tell him your love won't die
This heart of mine starts crying inside

You dream about him
Every dream about him
Well I'll be dreaming too
I'll be dreaming about you

Lyrics & Music by Leroy Lovett
With help from Harvey Sheldon

Edith Music Inc. copyright 1961

STAY AS BEAUTIFUL AS YOU ARE

Stay, as beautiful as you are
Remembering you as you were
Your memory has so many pages
Memories that seem to multiply
Just thinking of you as you were

Stay, as beautiful as you are
Remembering the good time we had
The romantic nights we shared
As we parted finding myself sad
Knowing I will never see you again

Without you sunrises never rises
Magnificent sunsets are not the same
I have survived with you amorous memories
Seeing you again as the sunrises
The sunsets will be magnificent

Now entering the autumn of my life
The seasons come as the years have
Finding you, seeing you would only be a miracle
We would meet, again it would be a miracle
Stay as beautiful as you are

Lyrics: Harvey Sheldon
Music: Leroy Lovett
Copyright 2001

THE ROAD

It was with hope and regret that I left Philadelphia. I had my whole life waiting ahead of me, but Philly was my home. I had always known that my choice of career meant I was going to hit the road, and I always wondered if I would ever end up back where I planted my roots.

Boston was quite a bit different than Philly. I started to see life speed up a bit more, and I felt like I was living in a real city, one without the small town feel I was used to back at home. My radio station license went through after a few legalities were taken care of, and I was soon broadcasting. In my travels I had met Roy Cohn, the famous lawyer during the McCarthy hearings, and made mention that I would like to make the move from talent to ownership one day in radio. He pulled a couple of strings for me and helped me ease my way into management. I've never been a great businessman, but when I smell an opportunity I've always been ready to take on the challenge.

Within a year, I had picked up another radio station in Miami and applied for and become the youngest owner of a television station in the country. I was only twenty-four years old, and I had two radio stations and a TV station in my portfolio. Plus, I could see the FM radio band coming. I was so impressed by the superior sound signal of FM over AM, that I jumped right in and was the first radio station to broadcast music on the FM dial. Up until then, FM band was like short wave radio is now. It was just a bunch of oddities on the air with no real reason behind it. I thought it was obviously a better way to broadcast music, but I was in the minority for quite awhile.

The Bunny Hop

I hadn't dated for awhile, because I was too busy working. I didn't have time for all the details I had previously spent so much energy on, only to come up empty. I had such a hectic schedule, I felt like I didn't have time to cram anything else into my calendar.. I started to take an interest in politics. Previously, all I cared about was entertainment, but I had built up a talk-radio type show in Boston where I had guests on. Some of the topical discussions got pretty heated. I led a battle to have the guilty verdict overturned for a man I felt was wrongfully imprisoned. I sensed the power of the media could be used for much more than helping make new music popular.

I had one guest on my show with whom I disagreed on just about everything, but he was so passionate and powerful that I felt transfixed by him. I had never met anyone as eloquent, even if I thought his brilliance was a bit misguided at the time. His name was Malcolm Little, and he was a self-driven disciple of Islam. He had yet to fully realize his powers or his real name. I watched with pride as Malcolm X confronted America one on one. I even had him over to my house for dinner once, where we finally found something we could agree upon. Both Muslims and Jews are not supposed to eat pork. I loved those battles on air, and I think I won a couple here and there. It gave me a real taste for politics, something I thought I might be able to pursue one day if I ever wanted to get out of the entertainment business. But, I was having too much fun to get that serious.

A friend of mine asked me to join him for a day at the beach, and I decided to make it an easy day and tag along. What I didn't know was that day would change my life in the best way possible. I was just walking along the beach when a young girl came over to me and asked me if I wanted to meet a nice, young Jewish girl who had just come back from Israel. She was talking about her cousin, Vivian Margolis. I agreed, figuring it would be fun, so why not? I wasn't going to dress up this time; I was going casual. I wasn't going to lay it on thick like I used to. I was going just relax and have some fun. Viv took my breath away as soon as I saw her, and we hit it off perfectly. I didn't have the age difference to worry about this time. We were both adults, and I felt comfortable immediately. I used to get kidded by my buddies, especially Clay Cohen, who noticed that I had a thing for look-a-likes. I used to explain to people what people looked like by comparing them to someone they would recognize. Usually, people would see the similarities instantly. My mother looked like Alice Faye in her youth, Dimples looked like Lauren Bacall, Marsha looked like Kim Novak, and Vivian looked like Jacqueline Kennedy. Being from Boston, she sounded a lot like her, too.

We met at a local drive-in restaurant that was running a promotion. If you said "Wo Wo Ginsburg," the name of a prominent radio DJ, you would get a free hamburger. I kept tapping the microphone and saying "Wo Wo Ginsburg." A waitress showed up with bags full of hamburgers. There had to be about twenty of them, but Viv wouldn't even have one, because they weren't kosher. I knew I found a winner.

I was fascinated by her, and we took off on a wonderful whirlwind romance that put all of my past romances to shame. I was ready to get married, and after twice thinking I had met the girl of my dreams, I knew I hadn't until then. Vivian was perfect for me. She was relaxed, confident, gorgeous, intelligent and above all, patient. I gave her a hundred reasons why she would have trouble with me. I told her how transient the business I was in was; I told her I might get rich and in no time be broke. I said I might have to move from job to job in a hurry and that my goal was still to get a network job. I would drop anything from anywhere to get to a better job. None of this scared Viv. She just kept on smiling and said she was willing to go wherever we had to. I met her on Mother's Day; we became engaged in September, and we were married in November of 1962.

The wedding was a typical Jewish wedding, with lots of food, celebration, and joy for everyone involved. I sat back and let everybody else take care of the details for a change. I only had one request. I wanted to pick the band. I didn't want a soft, old Jewish band up there going through the same old numbers in a really tired way. I wanted a band that could swing. I found the George Graham band and asked George if he wouldn't mind calling himself "Tito Schwartz" for a day so I could convince the elders to accept my conditions. He laughed and agreed, and he played great! Before you knew it, we were back from a brief honeymoon and headed to Florida to take care of a business opportunity that had opened up down there.

I was headed to Miami to look after my TV investment. I thought this would be a long run, based on how hard television stations were to get a hold of, and I was convinced I would have a license to print money in no time. But just as I started to feel comfortable, the same hand that had helped me got caught up in a huge legal scandal. Some radio and television stations were on the verge of falling into dangerous hands at that time, and the FCC didn't want the mafia or any other shady organization getting anywhere near the airwaves. I sensed the heat and liquidated my assets. I was investigated by the FCC, which was also hot on the trail of Jimmy Hoffa and the Teamsters. I hadn't committed any crimes and was cleared. I decided to go west.

I had my voice and my looks, so I always knew there would be a chance for me. I ended up in Fresno, California on KIAL, and I had a very successful television talk show that drew some big numbers. I was getting very adept at switching among politics, talk, and music. Then, I picked up another sidelight. I started doing sports. I found it a welcome relief. There was very little room for my *shtick* during the political debates, and there was not enough time as a DJ to tell stories, but in sports everybody has stories and loves to tell them. I fit right in.

By the mid-sixties, I had a pretty impressive résumé, but felt I wasn't getting the credit I deserved for some of my innovations. I pleaded with many station owners to give me a shot at being a general manager and letting me program the station. I finally got my wish on KLFM 105.5 FM in Long Beach. I wanted to put rock and roll music on FM radio twenty-four hours a day, something that had not been done yet. I even threw in some of my comedy routines. I broadcast my show six nights a week from the lounge of the Lafayette Hotel and usually drew quite a crowd. By now, Viv and I had started a family, and of all the places we'd been, I knew that she and the kids would want to end up in Southern California.

I got brave and threw my hat into the ring for a run at a state senate seat. I was going to walk the walk and talk the talk. I had the backing of the powerful Walter Knott (Knott's Berry Farms) and proper financing to get the job done. While I was campaigning and working my ass off at the radio station, I had a surprise visitor. It was Liz Renay, Mickey Cohen's girlfriend. I had both Liz and Mickey on my radio shows many times back in Philly and was friendly with them. She had just gotten out of prison in Terminal Island, where she served two years for perjury for protecting Mickey while in court.

We got to talking, and soon enough I figured out why she was visiting my show. She had the financing for a movie and asked me if I would co-star in it with her.

What's that saying? "Be careful what you ask for. You just might get it."

What I wanted all my life was finally mine for the taking. Of course I wanted to do it and finally get up on that big silver screen I'd worshipped all my life. I knew my chances of getting a network job were getting slimmer by the day but I had to take into account all that was around me. I would have had to quit my radio job, give up my senate campaign, and figure out a way to earn enough money to feed five. Then, when it was all over, I'd have to start all over again. The offer for the movie was six figures, and it sure was tempting. I thought that some of the money might be Mickey's, and that he could be wanting to give me a break I had waited for all of my life. I stared at the deal with all my heart and soul and finally said, "No." It wasn't what Mickey or anyone else wanted to hear, and the whole deal fell apart. Luckily, I had made the right decision.

I was projected as the winner in the open race for a new state senate seat and had the endorsement of Alex Drier, a major network TV newsman at the time. I had dined and drawn the support of a lot of Republicans, and I met a lot of great people during the campaign, including George Murphy, the Lodge family, Ronald Reagan, and George Dukukmejian. I knew that when I won I would join their club and really have a chance to make a difference.

I lost by just one hundred votes in one of the closest elections in history. KLFM had been sold, and the new owners of the station didn't like my asking price. So, I was fired.

This was the first time Viv stood up and said we had to get more serious about finding a place to plant roots and stay. She'd seen plenty of the road and was fond of Southern California, and I was too. So, what did I do? I took a job in St. Louis, where I had great numbers, and I started a hard rock, heavy metal type show that was quite popular. That lasted all of six months. I called in some of my connections in Philly and had a short run at WDAS, and then I ended up on WNAR, which was sold. After they were sold, they offered me a job at their sister

The Bunny Hop

station in the Tampa/St. Petersburg market in Florida. I flourished in the sunny climate of Florida and ended up doing talk radio. I also got a slot on the ABC affiliate there.

I had my best ratings ever in St. Pete, where I hit some big numbers. Strangely, I was seen on one of my TV broadcasts by the very people who made me the movie offer, and this time they wanted to talk about doing a movie about the Four Lads and the Philly connection. While we were talking over lunch about the project, I saw the FBI come in and wheel out two very wanted suspects in a mafia sting. Once again, I was a little too close to the action. The movie was never made, but I still had very high visibility in town as I added the role of columnist to my résumé by contributing to the Tampa Tribune. This run ended just like all the others when I was let go. I survived another year in the area being hired as a talk radio host in Jacksonville, where I never did get on the air. Instead, I just ended up selling advertising. The writing was on the wall; I was washed up, and we were tired of moving, so we went back to the San Diego area. There, my health started to suffer.

I had terrible headaches in my twenties and felt some odd pain for years, but I thought it was just stress, because no doctor could diagnose anything else. I went through the lowest part of my life and slipped out of my favored profession. My kids didn't really know about my radio and TV days, because they were too young. What they noticed was the way I moped around the house, depressed beyond belief. I was totally miserable, and if Vivian hadn't stuck by me, I never would have made through this *drek* alive. I was about as low as I could get when one day, my son asked me what was wrong.

I told him about my past, all my years in broadcasting, and how much I loved it. I was sad because I was forced to make a living doing something I dreaded, daily. Plus, I was horrible at it! He asked me what it would take to get back into the business, and I told him I'd need to make a demo. He asked how much a demo tape would cost to make, and I just blurted out, "50 dollars," guessing that's what it would cost to produce a little sample of my work, including the postage to send it around to some stations.

The next day, my son turned up with fifty dollars he'd saved from his paper route. When he gave it to me, I didn't know what to say, because I was so embarrassed. But, I felt that if he had showed that much faith in me. I needed to show the same for myself. I made a demo tape, dug out some addresses from an industry trade magazine, and sent the tapes out. Remarkably, within a few weeks, I had a talk radio show in San Diego and was back to my beloved broadcasting.

I started to make a nice living again by using my experience to do everything from heavy metal radio, to sports talk, to live reporting and eventually cable broadcasting. I was grateful that I had successfully re-invented myself at least two dozen times and had the chance to finally really enjoy my family and my life. We'd ended years of being on the road and had finally settled in Southern California for good.

Then, the headaches started to come roaring back. I finally found a specialist, Dr. Martin Harvey Weiss at USC, who properly diagnosed my illness. I had a brain tumor that had been growing for years behind my eyes. I was scheduled for surgery, and while I was waiting, I taped a whole bunch of shows in hopes that I could generate some income while I was laid up.

The prognosis wasn't good. The physician who was going to perform the surgery told me I had less than a fifty-percent chance of keeping my eyesight. I was scared to death. How could I support my family? What would I be able to do for a living? I was convinced I was going to be blind, and I prayed more than I ever had.

When I woke up, I decided I would try to open one eye at a time. I opened my left eye: Total darkness. I hesitated and prepared myself for the worst. I opened my right eye, and I could feel the light. I had some vision. Not a lot, but some. Slowly, my sight came back. The tumors had rested against my optic nerve, making the operation very dangerous and delicate. To make my life even more complicated, the surgeon decided to try a new technique and do all of his work by entering through my nose to get at the tumor, instead of going in through the top of my skull. I didn't enjoy the after effects, but I am forever grateful that he had the touch of a magician. I made up my mind that I was one lucky son of a gun to be alive and well, and I promised God that I would spend the rest of my days being the best person I could be.

THE SEARCH

I had heard that there was going to be a Bandstand Anniversary, but I didn't know how or when the celebration would occur. The Bunny Hop had been such a big part of the show and the whole Philly scene, that I thought it would be featured prominently in the occasion. It made me think. Where had Dimples been over all these years, and how had her life gone? I had lost track of her, and there was no way she could have ever followed my long and winding trail across America. The last time I had seen her was at a restaurant in Philadelphia a few years after our Bandstand days, but now as we both approached sixty years of age, I barely knew where to start looking. I really did want to find her.

I wondered how to find somebody when you only know her nickname. I didn't know her birthday; I couldn't remember her first name, her last name, or her maiden name. I just knew her as Dimples. I didn't know where she lived. Then, one day I saw an ad on TV by The Search Company. They promoted a service claiming that they could find old acquaintances, relatives, and friends. So I called them up. I thought "Hell; I've got nothing to lose."

They asked if I knew her name. I said no. Did I know where she lived? I said no. All of my answers were no. They told me the task was impossible. I really wanted them to take my case, but all I could tell them was that her name was Dimples, she went to Lincoln High School, and she had once lived in the Oxford Circle section of town, where I had grown up. After some convincing, they started up on this impossible search.

Their first clue was very misleading. There were sixteen people in Pennsylvania that had Dimples as nicknames, and they had various last names. But, I didn't know her last name. So, we thought there might be some leads in the old article in the Philadelphia Inquirer that showed the Bunny Hop steps to a national audience in 1953. I contacted the Temple University archives, where I found the original photographs and the article. To our delight, the original story had both our given names and the physical addresses where we lived, which is something no newspaper would dare print today. Her real name turned out to be Erma Eineger. With that clue, I was told all I needed was her birth date. Then, the search would be considerably narrowed.

I called up the principal of Lincoln High School. I felt odd about calling, because the last time I came in contact with the headmaster, I was getting tossed out of school. I made a remark to that effect to break the ice. I also felt compelled to convince the fine administrator that I wasn't some sort of stalker. He was very cordial and asked what warranted my expulsion. I confessed that I wasn't up for the fine cuisine in the cafeteria. Therefore, I had walked across the street to get a good lunch and subsequently been caught. "That's it?" the principal asked incredulously. "We'd love to have students today with that as their biggest crime!" We became friendly, and I told him about the search for Dimples. I mentioned the "blue card" collection, where they kept all of the student's records on file, and he promised to get back to me the next day. Sure enough, he was a man of his word, and he called back to give me Dimples's birthday. I quickly called up The Search Company, and they said that the birthday was all they would need in order to find her.

I let go a great sigh of relief, but my anticipation grew. I had done all that I could, and I trusted the people at The Search Company to do the rest. When I called the next day, I felt sure they would have a phone number or an address where I could contact Dimples.

I kept thinking back to a particular conversation Dimples and I had near the time I was leaving Bandstand to go to my radio gig. She had always wanted to be in show business, mostly as a dancer, and would try very hard to achieve that goal. I was equally determined to make a name for myself in the entertainment business. At our last talk on the set, I confessed and told her that I would never forget her, and that in every article I would always mention her when asked about the Bunny Hop. I felt I had honored that promise, and I wanted to make sure she knew it. Then, the researchers called.

"Yes, Harvey," the spokesman said over the phone. "We have some information for you on Dimples." I jumped for joy, but before I could ask, "When can I speak to her?" they continued, "She's passed away."

I was stunned. I couldn't move. I couldn't talk. I could barely stand up. How in God's name could this happen? This can't be! I was devastated. I thanked the company for their services and politely asked then to send me the bill for their time.

For two years, we had made numerous phone call inquiries, all knowing that the search was going to be difficult. In the end, I never considered the fact that Dimples could be gone. She was too young! I felt like I had lost my mother or my sister. Although we had lost touch over the years, that was how emotionally connected I was. Those days on Bandstand were my defining moment. The pain got worse when I scoured my deepest inner thoughts. I had a feeling that she didn't have a happy life. I hadn't thought much of the jock she was dating in high school. He was insanely jealous about our dancing partnership on Bandstand, and I just didn't think he was right for her. I was praying that my instincts were wrong, but in my heart I knew I was right. If only I could make it up to her! Now she was gone, and I moped about for days afterwards, grieving in my own way. All the attention focused on Bandstand seemed like a distant event, as my thoughts kept drifting back to Dimples.

Oddly, one day The Search Company called me back and told me that they had contacted Crook & Chase's syndicated TV show. They had shown keen interest in my story about the Bunny Hop and the Bandstand years and wanted me to appear on their program. The Search Company waived their retainer fee, saying that the publicity generated would be great for their business. I gladly accepted. I was still feeling at a loss knowing that Dimples wouldn't be there, and I had a month to go over the scenario in my mind. I asked God in my prayers, "Is it possible that they made a mistake?" Maybe they got the wrong gal?

I kept bugging the company to keep investigating. Somehow, I could not accept the fact that she had passed on. I always wanted to show her that I kept my promise, and that whenever asked about the Bunny Hop, I had always spoken of her to make sure that she received full credit for what she had accomplished. I wanted to share that joy with her, even if we would never meet again.

On the day of the show, I felt like shit. I felt empty. Half of the Bunny Hop team was missing, and I didn't feel like I deserved all the credit. If I could have walked away and cancelled the whole show without anybody knowing, I would have easily made that call.

I was as nervous as hell sitting in the dressing room in the back parking lot. When the program taping began, I tried to compose myself as best I could and not let on how much I was suffering inside. I went onto the show, and it was a very flattering. I relaxed a little because of the friendly dialogue of quick and insightful questions between the hosts and the guest. I did my best to keep the pace sharp. Thoughtfully, The Search Company, who worked so diligently on my behalf, came out and did some explaining of their efforts.

They admitted to us that they had indeed found a death certificate for Erma Eineger, but also added, "Dimples has left a message for you, Harvey."

My thoughts flew all over, and I could barely keep my wits. I was hoping it wouldn't be something that would upset my wife, because I'd always been honest with Viv about Dimples. I couldn't believe all the different scenarios that were racing through my brain as I sat there on television. Would the message be bad or good? I just did not know what to think. It had to be positive because I always thought of Dimples as a real sweetheart and not one who could ever say anything rude or destructive about another person. I took a deep breath and relaxed, finally letting my emotions run full circle. At the very least, it would be some kind of closure, and I could accept what the truth was. Then, we took a four-minute commercial break that felt like an hour. It was way too long to be left alone in thought.

After that eternity ended, Diana from The Search Company said, "Actually, Harvey, Dimples didn't leave you a message."

We turned to the side and focused our attention on the divider.

Then I heard the words, "Ladies and gentlemen, here's Dimples!"

My jaw dropped, and I thought my eyes were going to fly out of my head! She's alive! Quickly, I had to put forty-five years of time in perspective to recognize her face, as I'm sure she would have done when she saw me. I thought she was probably thinking, "Boy, he's lost it. look at those extra pounds!" We condensed nearly a half-century worth of memories in microseconds on a television show, and all I could do was stare across the room. I was afraid to blink my eyes. I did not want to lose sight of this spectacle. My throat was as dry as could be, and I felt like I was immediately cast in marble. Had I moved any less, they would have had to reclassify me as a statue!

It really was Dimples. I embraced her, holding on hard. I felt flush and tried as hard as I could to compose myself. She looked great and was shy in front of the cameras as Crook and Chase helped us reminisce about the old Bandstand days, the days that were such a dramatic highlight in both our lives. Of course, they had the music, and as the familiar notes from Ray Anthony's song came out of the studio speakers, we were asked to demonstrate the steps. Dimples still had the moves. I was like the old athlete who had "lost a step." Even with two left feet, nothing was going to diminish this moment. We laughed as the cameras faded and our segment of the TV show was over. I was eternally grateful to the Search Company, Crook and Chase, and all the wonderful people who had put this day together.

Slowly, I got to put the whole scenario together. During the search the researchers had mistakenly identified Dimples as the deceased, when in fact it was her mother. They both had the same birth name, but Erma Eineger had changed her name to Dedi MacGregor. Her husband at the time grew weary of the name Dimples and what it implied. When she married, she took his last name of MacGregor, and changed her first name to Dedi. When Dimples got word that I had been looking for her, she called their number, and sensing the drama of the whole episode, the Search Company contacted the TV show and helped put it all together. All the while, they kept it a surprise for me!

Afterwards, Dimples and I had a lot of catching up to do. I asked if she was going to stay a couple of days. I really wanted her to meet my wife and my family. After all, they had heard so much about her, and I knew they would really enjoy meeting her. Politely, she declined, and I had to ask why. I was actually shocked to hear her answer.

She said, "I didn't expect you to be so nice." I was taken aback.

"Wasn't I nice back in the Bandstand days?"

"Of course, you were," she said. "I just assumed that after all these years, you would be traveling in different company, and I wouldn't feel comfortable."

That remark had some history behind it. Sure, Dimples and I were a great couple on TV, but we did come from different social strata, and our crowds rarely associated with each other. I had to ask.

"Dimples," I said, "If I had asked you for a date back in the Bandstand days, would you have gone out with me?"

"No way!" she said instantly. I asked why.

"We were from different crowds, and it wouldn't have worked out. Plus, I was going steady with my boyfriend." From there, Dimples opened up. She confirmed my fears that she had a rough life. Her boyfriend became her husband, and they had a son right after they were married. Her husband was a boozer and an abuser. After too many beatings, she left him and raised her son alone, but she never remarried because of her father's strict religious beliefs. She worked hard, most of the time taking two jobs to make ends meet, and she lived a simple life. When she got the call from Crook and Chase about the show, she initially turned down the offer, thinking it would be too embarrassing or difficult for her. Finally, she was convinced to go, and I'm so glad she did.

They flew her out first class, put her up in a fancy hotel, had her make-up done by a glamorous Hollywood stylist, and treated her like a queen. The show was great for both of us, and I wanted to spend more time with Dimples, but I would only have the forty-five minutes it took to get to the airport, so she could catch her flight back home. During the drive she kept insisting that she had no idea that I would be so nice. I felt flattered, but a bit confused. After all those years between us, we both had misconceptions that had to be proved untrue. She had thought that I would be aloof and arrogant, traits that showbusiness people could easily be accused of. I certainly had been humbled enough not to fall into that trap, and I think it surprised her. As we walked through the airport, our conversation deepened.

"This trip has been wonderful," she said. "They treated me so incredibly well. I've never flown first class before. The hotel was lovely, the beautician was amazing, and the television show certainly was everything I ever dreamed it could have been."

Then she confessed.

"Harvey," she said, "This was the greatest day of my life."

I was so happy for her, I felt tears well up in my eyes. She continued as we walked through LAX.

"My mother always said, 'Someday you will see Harvey Sheldon again.' I'm so glad I did." We hugged, and before she had to go, I needed to express my feelings.

"I will never lose you again, Dimples." She started to lose it a bit, so I had to find the lighter side of the moment. "You're too hard to find!" We both got a laugh out of that. I told her I would be in Philadelphia later in the year, and we would spend some time together and catch up. I knew she thought it would be just some empty promise that wouldn't come true, but I did look her up when I got back to Philly. We went to meet some of my friends in the media, and she loved every minute of it. I don't think through all those years either of us had a true grasp on what we had cooked up in that community room at Lincoln High School. We found out that the Bunny Hop music score, with us dancing on the cover, was in the Smithsonian Museum.

"Didn't I keep my promise?" I asked. "Every time I was asked about the Bunny Hop, I always mentioned you and insisted that your name be in the story."

"Yes, you did Harvey." she said. "Every time." That's when she told me she had kept a scrapbook of all the articles she had seen of me in the press over the years. That made me feel like a million dollars.

REDEMPTION

I never became the network TV personality I wanted to be. I got a few minor roles on national TV shows and did a lot of regional television and radio shows. I even put together a syndicated cable TV show, but let's face it, I never was a star or you would have heard of me! That's all right, though. The reason it is so hard to become a star, is because so many people want to be one. If it were so easy, a lot more people would have made it. The true lesson in my journey through life is that you have to try. I brag to my friends that I have never worked a day in my life. It's a bit of a stretch, but I never considered being on the airwaves to be work. It was pleasurable to me. I made up my mind at a very early age that I would chase my dream, no matter what the price and no matter where it took me. I feel that I put up a good effort.

If I hadn't left my native Philadelphia, I could never have met God's greatest gift to me in my life, my wife Vivian. We've had three children, a grandchild, and a wonderful time together, despite my hectic career. She's been by my side through everything. It was so hard making plans or raising children when getting uprooted so often. Her never-ending tolerance, patience, love, and understanding have been my greatest support. She's been an unbelievable wife, mother, friend, and hostess. We've entertained some incredible people in our home, including Malcolm X, Mort Sahl, Ralph Nader, Larry Parks, Betty Garrett, George Murphy, Sam Levinson, and Dr. Carlton Fredericks. Viv handled it all with ease. She even came up with a couple of one-liners that I get good mileage out of.

The Bunny Hop

Harvey Sheldon lecturing on the history of Jewish American Music in Philadelphia at the University of Pennsylvania. 2004

REDEMPTION

One time, when we were in the South, we were at a banquet where we met Lester Maddox. We were seated at the same table, and when the famed race-bating former governor offered my wife some fruit, she politely declined by saying, "From you, Governor, never!" Another time, we were in St. Louis at a function when President Lyndon Johnson just kept staring at her. He was absolutely convinced Jacqueline Kennedy was in the room. He sent over a couple of secret service agents to get a better look. When they came over, Viv laid the Boston accent on real thick and they wouldn't give up the chase until she was forced to show them her photo I.D. I still think my greatest accomplishment in life is my marriage to Vivian.

I have been so blessed. Every time I have faced a crisis, a new opportunity has arisen, and that still continues today. I still think about my temporary blindness and how close I came to going blind permanently. I try to live up to my promise to God every day. In my latter years, with all the kids off on their own, Viv and I have settled in Orange County, south of Los Angeles, and we live a comfortable life. I have spent most of my time working on projects I feel are worthy and philanthropic. I have amassed a huge collection of films and videos. For decades, the record companies have been sending me masters of their promotional and for-sale videos. I saved them all, and in many cases, I have videos those same record companies have lost or destroyed. I have used this library to make a buck here and there, but after a lot of soul searching, I figured out what to do with them.

The production of rock videos has been where the majority of new techniques in directing and shooting film have occurred. There are a couple of reasons why. The artists who create the music have vivid imaginations, and the directors they have worked with have had both the vision and the budget to pull it off. In submitting these mini-films to MTV and other cable outlets, this generation of filmmakers has influenced the way movies are made. Now, most movies look like giant MTV epics. I had my collection appraised and decided to donate it to the University of Southern California, if they would make these films available for study. In effect, we were creating the world's first rock and roll video library, and they asked me if I would mind if they named the library after me. I was flattered.

After years of producing rock and roll and heavy metal video shows for cable networks, I have gone back to my first love: The big band scene. Currently, I produce a regular video show that I have a lot of fun doing, even if I don't make much money putting it together. I do it because it's what I love to do. The big band show has created a lot of opportunities. When the American Music Festival decided to do a search for the one hundred greatest songs of the twentieth century, I was added as their chief historian. Recently, Clive Davis, one of the true visionaries in the music business, asked me to put together the definitive big band show for their new Internet venture. None of these opportunities would have appeared, if I hadn't taken a chance.

When Jon and I started working on this book, we had some interest. We even had a movie agent give us a call, but then, all the action stopped. It would have been easy just to let the book go and move on to new adventures. My hope was diminishing, but I knew there was a way to keep my dream alive. One night, I was thinking about my old mafia buddy, Angelo. I had heard from my friends that a few years ago, he had been gunned down by some bitter rivals. I still thought of him often. He was such an influence on my life.

He told me he would always be there when I needed him, and I felt in this moment of despair that it was time to reach out. I found myself talking out loud. "I don't know if you are in heaven or hell, Angelo, but I really could use your help right now." Sure enough, the next day we got the break we needed to get this book published.

While doing our research and gathering all of the information we needed to put in this book, I started to think about my old friends a lot more. I tried to follow most of their exploits, but many have died or gone on to another line of work, or I have lost track of them the same way I did with Leroy Lovett. Every time I went back to Philly, I'd always ask, "Where's Leroy Lovett?" Nobody seemed to know, but when I started working on the book, all of a sudden, I got Leroy's phone number. It turns out he lives right here in Southern California, and we caught up on a lot of good times. Leroy found the sheet music to the songs we wrote together and now intends to record them, forty years after they were written! He wants me to collaborate with him on a new musical based on these songs. Fantastic!

I have used my expertise on American music to lecture at a local state university. I put together a classy little production full of my *shtick*

REDEMPTION

and some great footage. I get rave reviews every time I get a chance to lecture. Now, I'm getting invitations from all over the country to take this show on the road. I always wanted to make a contribution in Philadelphia, where it all started. I wanted to donate my entire collection of American music footage, over 4,500 titles, to the University of Pennsylvania, where it could be preserved forever. I had the collection appraised at four million dollars. It took three years to work out all the arrangements, but finally, the university accepted the donation and decided to name the facility the Harvey Sheldon Jewish-American Music Video Research Library. I was thrilled and humbled.

I was invited to the dedication of the musical museum and looked forward to another great trip back to my hometown. I was saddened that I couldn't convince anybody in my family to go with me. To them, this was old news. I, However, was ecstatic, so I flew east solo. When I arrived, there were articles in all the major papers, and Fox News picked up the story for the evening broadcast the day of the ceremony. I couldn't help but feel alone. I had labored for years to put this collection, which I know is the finest in the world, together. Now I have an Ivy League university that has named a library after me, and I'm standing backstage alone. It made me nostalgic.

I thought about Angelo Bruno, and all he did for me. I thought about my career and all the friends I had made over the years. I never felt so alone. Then, I thought a little applause might cheer me up.

I heard the beginning of my introduction, and a female voice sounded familiar, but I couldn't place it. I racked my brain trying to remember who it was, but it had been at least forty years. I moved closer to the stage, flattered by the warm remarks I was receiving. Finally, I had to look. It was Marsha!

She looked ravishing, and little had I known, she had become very active in community affairs and had volunteered, unbeknownst to me, to be my presenter. I walked towards her, and we embraced. I whispered in her ear, "I never forgot you," and she confided in me, "I missed you terribly."

After the presentation, Marsha and I went out to our favorite Italian restaurant, and we reminisced for hours. It felt like old times, and I promised Marsha that I would keep in touch and look her up every time I came to Philly. The evening that started out so poorly had inspired me to return to my roots. Marsha asked me to compose another song, and I wrote the first line on a napkin: "Stay as beautiful as you are."

I don't know what it is about Philadelphia and the Bunny Hop, but they have rewarded me over and over all my life. It made me think of where it all started. I thought back to that aptitude test I took as a kid, which determined I should be a rabbi. The true meaning of the word "rabbi," in Hebrew, is teacher, and I'm being asked to teach, so they were right. I have come full circle.

My life has been a complex journey, with many up and downs. Some were successes, and a lot were failures. I'm proud of the many things I have accomplished, and I've tried my hardest to chase my dreams. It's like an expression they use in sports, "Make sure you leave it all on the field." I have, and I will keep on going until God calls for my soul.

Harvey Sheldon hosting a syndicated TV show, "Monster Rock" a heavy metal show. 1996

Harvey Sheldon in his TV production studio producing one of hs video lectures 2005

GLOSSARY OF WORDS WE USED

YIDDISH — ENGLISH

Yiddish	English
balebosteh	homemaker
bissal	softer
boitshick	affectionate for boy or man
chutzpeh	guts, balls
drek	crap, shit
frailech	a festive happy dance
kasheh	a mess
k'vetsh	whine
mazal tov	a celebration
mensch	a fine gentleman
phakata	shit
pishechtz	piss
schmoozen	mingle, negotiate
schmuck	idiot
schpeal	plea
shaineh maidel	beautiful lady
shikker	drunkard
shulfights	Jewish dance
simcheh	party
stchooped	kick
shtick	my thing
touche	ass
tshepen	annoying

Harvey Sheldon and his wife Vivian of 45 years. 2005

HARVEY SHELDON

Entertainment industry veteran Harvey Sheldon has assembled a series of highly entertaining and educational series of lectures with video illustration detailing the important but little-appreciated story. How the founding fathers of American music, most of them immigrants of Russian-Jewish extraction, created the American songbook, jazz, the Broadway musical, as well as the radio, recording and the movie industries.

Sheldon, a born entertainer and story-teller, has studied this era of Americana closely. His series of presentations draw upon the video libraries of Jewish-American music he has donated to the University of Pennsylvania and University of Southern California. These shows captivate audiences, hold them spellbound, teach important lessons about American Jewish culture, and capture the immigrant experience. His question-and-answer sessions always go overtime because the audiences do not want to leave.

Multimedia footage includes seldom-seen performances by Al Jolson, Alice Faye, Judy Garland, Lena Horne, Eddie Cantor, Cab Calloway, Doris Day, Benny Goodman, Artie Shaw, Harry James and many, many more, performing the timeless music of Jerome Kern, George Gershwin, Rodgers and Hart, Rodgers and Hammerstein, Harold Arlen, and others inspired by them. Audiences are spellbound, educated and are entertained by the most creative period in American music history. Harvey Sheldon's timeless presentation is a must see for anyone interested in 'emmis' (the truth) behind the growth of America's greatest export: music and the roles of the Jews who helped create this fantastic art form.

For further information about Harvey Sheldon's video lecture series please contact:

THE EMMIS FOUNDATION
Preserving the Jewish-American Music History
7855 East Horizon View Drive
Anaheim Hills, CA 92808
T/F-714-281-5929
e-mail:harveysheldontv@hotmail.com
website: www.harveysheldontv.com

ABOUT THE AUTHOR

JON SUTHERLAND

Jon Sutherland is a free-lance journalist who has written columns, features, and cover stories that have appeared in over sixty magazines world-wide. His credits range from *Runner's World* to *Metal Hammer*. Jon's primary journalistic interests are athletics and music. He is the co-author of *Boulevard of Broken Dreams: The Hanoi Rocks Story*, *The Bunny Hop: The Harvey Sheldon Story and the Bandstand Years*. His latest book *Hey D.A.D. Thanks!*, is an intimate story of a son's appreciation for his father.

An avid distance runner, Jon has logged over 170,000 miles of running. He has won awards as a journalist and runner. He competed in athletics internationally and has not missed a day of running since May 25, 1969.

Jon Sutherland
24415 Vanowen St. #45
West Hills, CA 91307
jonrunrock@ aol.com

"A very special friend from my hometown, who has wit, style, and the gift to write like the big Broadway writers of yesterday: Rodgers, Gershwin, Hammerstein and Berlin. One look at the lyrics Harvey put to my music tells you Harvey is a winner."

Leroy Lovett
Composer
Duke Ellington collaborator

"As a \oung musician emerging on the scene in Philadelphia in the fifties and sixties, I remember fondly the thrilling sounds of Harvey Sheldon's Jazz Band."

Frank Leone
Former arranger for Paul Anka, Englebert Humperdink
President of Musicians Union of Las Vegas

"Philly's Harvey Sheldon rocks the philanthropic establishment by creating and donating the world's first rock and roll research video library at the University of Southern California."

Steve Feldman
Steve Feldman
Jewish Exponent

"The Bunny Hop is an exceptional read. Philadelphia was the capital of the music scene in the 1950s, and Harvey Sheldon was right in the middle of the action. The teenager convinced original Bandstand host Bob Horn to add dancers to the music show. Then, he and a girl nicknamed "Dimples" created a dance to the smash hit song, "The Bunny Hop." Soon, kids from all over the country were doing the dance perfected by Harvey and Dimples. Harvey Sheldon has spent more than 50 years in the entertainment business, and readers will love going down memory lane with him."

Tom Waring
The Times

Printed in the United States
43458LVS00006B/22-171